Praise for *Lucky I*

"I am a massive fan of Denise, her books, and her courses. Down to earth, honest, and at times hilarious, DDT shows us how to create a truly exceptional life."

REBECCA CAMPBELL, AUTHOR OF *LIGHT IS THE NEW BLACK* AND *RISE SISTER RISE*

"Denise is one of the world's best teacher on the Law of Attraction. Every day she impresses me with her wisdom, business savvy, integrity, and teachings."

LEONIE DAWSON, AUTHOR OF *LESSONS EVERY GODDESS MUST KNOW* AND THE *SHINING YEAR* WORKBOOKS

"Denise is the ultimate money mindset mentor. With her systems, tools, and tricks to open up your heart and mind to receive the abundance that is your birthright, you can't fail. Everybody needs some Denise in their life."

SUSIE MOORE, AUTHOR OF *WHAT IF IT DOES WORK OUT?*

"Denise is a refreshing voice on money mindset. She writes in a way that is easeful and humorous, and you'll feel like she's right there with you as you put her lessons to work and create a more abundant business and life."

NATALIE MACNEIL, AUTHOR OF *SHE TAKES ON THE WORLD* AND *THE CONQUER KIT*

Lucky Bitch

Also by Denise Duffield-Thomas

Get Rich, Lucky Bitch!

A GUIDE FOR
EXCEPTIONAL WOMEN
TO CREATE **OUTRAGEOUS**
SUCCESS

DENISE DUFFIELD-THOMAS

HAY HOUSE, INC.
Carlsbad, California • New York City
London • Sydney • New Delhi

Published in the United Kingdom by: Hay House UK, Ltd.,
The Sixth Floor, Watson House, 54 Baker Street, London W1U 7BU
Phone: +44 (0)20 3927 7290 • Fax: +44 (0)20 3927 7291
www.hayhouse.co.uk

Published in the United States of America by:
Hay House Inc., PO Box 5100, Carlsbad, CA 92018-5100
Tel: (1) 760 431 7695 or (800) 654 5126; Fax: (1) 760 431 6948 or (800) 650 5115
www.hayhouse.com

Published in Australia by:
Hay House Australia Ltd, 18/36 Ralph St, Alexandria NSW 2015
Tel: (61) 2 9669 4299; Fax: (61) 2 9669 4144; www.hayhouse.com.au

Published in India by:
Hay House Publishers India, Muskaan Complex, Plot No.3, B-2,
Vasant Kunj, New Delhi 110 070
Tel: (91) 11 4176 1620; Fax: (91) 11 4176 1630; www.hayhouse.co.in

Text © Denise Duffield-Thomas, 2012, 2018

Previously published by CreateSpace Independent Publishing Platform
(ISBN: 978-1-46632-224-0)

The moral rights of the author have been asserted.

The information given in this book should not be treated as
a substitute for professional medical advice; always consult a
medical practitioner. Any use of information in this book is at the
reader's discretion and risk. Neither the author nor the publisher
can be held responsible for any loss, claim or damage arising out
of the use, or misuse, of the suggestions made, the failure to take
medical advice or for any material on third party websites.

A catalogue record for this book is available from the British Library.

ISBN: 978-1-78817-132-8

Author photo p.269: Eyes of Love Photography, www.eyesoflove.com.au

Printed in the United States of America

11 10 9 8 7 6 5 4 3 2

Contents

Introduction

"The day you decide to do it is your lucky day."
JAPANESE PROVERB

*H*ey lucky lady! Today is *your* lucky day.

You're either reading this book because you're already quite lucky and you want to attract even more into your life, or you're thinking, *Are you kidding me? My luck has just about run out! What's wrong with me?* If it's the second option, you still have a tiny bit of hope – a voice inside that says, *This isn't all there is.*

Either way, get ready, because this little book will *blow your mind.* It has the potential to change your life, just like it's done for tens of thousands of women around the world. (I love it when self-help gurus make big promises like that, don't you?)

I'll be honest: not everything in this book is 100 percent new or ground-breaking, because – let's face it – there's really nothing new under the sun. After all, if you've ever read *any* personal development books, you've probably heard most of this before. You might, however, need to be reminded of what you already know – that you have the power to change your life, and that you 100 percent deserve your dreams.

The basics work, but hardly anyone really works the basics. And that's especially true for a "fuzzy" concept like the Law of Attraction.

However, in *Lucky Bitch*, you'll read *practical examples* of the Law of Attraction in action that might sound like magic on the surface. Keep reading though: every story in this book (including my own) is completely true and unembellished, even if it sounds *unbelievable* at first. You'll see how, when you deconstruct success, hardly anything is random "luck."

And you'll learn, step by step, exactly what you can do to replicate these success stories in your own life.

Have you ever thought, *You lucky bitch!* about a friend or someone you've seen on TV? I have – and I still sometimes think that, especially when I forget that I have the power to manifest amazing results for myself. Jealousy is normal, and it usually shows up when you're ready for more in your life. You have to be prepared to see it as a good sign, though, and *do* something about it; because becoming the green-eyed monster is not cute at all.

Are you ready for more?

Whether you're "naturally lucky" or not, by the end of this book, you'll be fully embracing your absolutely *awesome* good fortune. Plus, you'll be surprised how easy it can be to create your own version of a First-class life.

The truth is that we can *all* consciously create good luck in our own lives. And we can do it not just through hard work and perspiration (as the saying goes), but by combining the *right* kind of effort with an unwavering belief that we deserve to experience the highest levels of love, abundance, good health, and personal success – regardless of our current circumstances.

If other people can do it, why not you?

When you realize this, the results can be astounding. Such amazing things can come into your life that you might think, *OMG, what's happening?!*

So even though I call myself "the Lucky Bitch," I want you to know the truth: I haven't been specially selected by the Universe. There's nothing particularly unusual about me: I wasn't born under a lucky star, I didn't grow up wealthy, and I haven't won the lottery. I'm smart, but I'm not a genius or anything. I'm just a normal chick like you.

Yes, I've created a multi-million-dollar business. I live a pretty chilled-out, successful life, too; and even though I teach personal development, I'm not even close to being perfect (I wish!). So please don't think I'm some out-of-touch "guru" telling you what to do.

I've achieved some awesome results in the last couple of years, but I still had to get over my fear of not being perfect before I wrote this book. I still yell at my husband when I've got PMS, I get a hangover after parties, and sometimes I even cheat at Scrabble. I'm just an imperfect human being, with faults like anyone else.

I also want you to know that, like many people, I didn't have the most auspicious start in life. In fact, there were many occasions in my life where I was downright *unlucky*. Times when I was literally down to my last dollar, when I struggled with finding a fulfilling job, and when I honestly felt like the huge potential inside me was being squandered. That's a painful feeling, right?

Once I made the decision to negotiate my reality (and believed I *deserved it*) though, the most extraordinary things started to happen. I became unbelievably lucky. Opportunities seemed to be attracted to me, and crazy synchronicities became a normal, everyday occurrence. I started seeing bank errors in my favor, winning all-expenses-paid travel around the world, and attracting the right mentors and courses – along with the money to pay for them. I even started winning at Bingo! It all seemed magical.

At first I thought it was random; but it happened with such regularity that I had to take a second look at what I was doing to attract all this good fortune.

I was always a personal development junkie, but nothing like *this* had ever happened to me before. I'd actually thought I was immune to the Law of Attraction up until this point. I'd been a regular attendee at some of the cheesiest personal development seminars, and was always reading goal-setting books... but it was hard work, and I couldn't figure out what I was doing "wrong." Was I not meditating hard enough? Did the Universe not like me? Maybe if I just lost ten pounds...?

At first, when I started studying the Law of Attraction, it was two steps forward, one step back... up until that one magical year, when everything I wanted suddenly came true. In fact, when I added up all of the unexpected gifts from the Universe that year, I realized they were worth *half a million dollars*, even though I had huge money blocks at the time.

I recorded everything I did to manifest my dreams during that year – especially all the really small, practical things – to come up with a blueprint I could replicate. Then I tested my concepts by coaching other women in similar situations. And, almost without fail, amazing things began happening to them, too.

I still get messages all the time now that start with, *"Denise, you're never going to believe what happened..."* Suddenly, ordinary women like you and me are attracting their dream clients, pay increases, free stuff, new relationships, and increased levels of happiness for no reason (at least, none the outside world could see). They're becoming more *attractive* to the Universe.

So what's going on?

Honestly – I think it's our time. The world around us is changing, especially for women. Many of us are awakening to the possibility of being the Directors of our own lives. We realize that we don't have to just accept what we're given. We realize that our reality is highly malleable. We realize that *we're* responsible for our own circumstances every day.

None of these revelations are new: we're simply remembering how powerful we are, and turning away from old belief systems, just like we'd shrug off last season's wine-stained coat. We don't have to live the same conventional life that other people do. We can choose to live an awesome life without guilt. That's the Lucky Bee (we don't call ourselves bitches) life.

It's so easy today to find the information we need to unlock these secrets and keep our positive vibrations high. New leaders are emerging to show us the way – you might even be one of them. Concepts like manifestation and the Law of Attraction have become more mainstream. Thanks to the power of the Internet, we can find our like-minded tribes worldwide, and share what we know with each other. Thank Goddess for this new age of technology, right?

I'm so grateful that I can be part of this movement – that I can be a living, breathing example of what you can do when you harness your own power and decide to live in your own reality. This is not a book where I just brag about my accomplishments and how astoundingly lucky I've become. Well, not... *entirely*. There IS a teeny, tiny amount of bragging, because I want to role model success for you and normalize this conversation. However, my genuine wish is that reading it inspires you to join the global Lucky Bee tribe, and become one of the women who's been able to harness this unbelievable luck for themselves. Because, trust me: it's not random.

This little book is also designed to inspire you to take action in areas of your life that may be lacking some magic. Some of the concepts in it might be familiar to you, and some may be new. Either way, I invite you to take them all to a new level, and manifest what you've always dreamed of in your life.

I want you to wonder: *what else could be possible?*

To help you with your manifesting, you'll learn some very practical techniques to exponentially increase your luck, and some woo-woo metaphysical concepts, too. Together, they'll produce amazing results in the *real world*, and make your day-to-day life much more fun and fulfilling.

However, you need to know that the results are not always 100 percent predictable. When you set an intention to change your life, it *will* happen. *Always*. Not always in the way you expected, but always in the way *you asked for*. That can create some pretty "out there" results if you're not good at asking for what you want. The Universe is ridiculously literal, so I've given you lots of trouble-shooting tips in this book.

Not only that, but the time frame for your desires to show up is also unpredictable. The Universe is a complex machine. No-one knows the exact chain of events that you put in motion when you send out a request to the Universe. You can only trust that you've been heard, and that you'll be taken care of. And, most importantly, you need to *do the work* so that the Universe can align itself to your desires. You might have to emotionally or physically declutter; and there could be other work that needs doing to make space for the good stuff to come through.

But trust me: if you do the work, the Universe *always* provides.

This can be tough to really *get* for some women. If you're not used to being looked after, or if you've had some challenges in your life, you're conditioned to expect the worst.

Maybe in the future, you won't need the rituals and techniques that I describe in this book in order to manifest your heart's desires. Maybe one day, you'll be able to manifest instantly through some freaky teleportation juju. In the meantime, though, you do need the techniques; perhaps as a pathway for you to believe you can actually do it. Future generations will probably laugh at our primitive rituals and our doubt that we really can direct our intentions to create what we want.

As you read this book, ask yourself constantly: *What do I really want for myself?* or *How can I apply this in my life?* Write down your thoughts in your journal, and review them often. I've also created a free action guide for you, so download it from www.DeniseDT.com/bonus and play along.

Some chapters might bring up some negative emotions for you, like disbelief or impatience that it's not happening quickly enough for you. If so, I get it. I've been there, girlfriend!

You might also experience frustration, anger or resentment (maybe even at me) as you read this book. If this happens, put your hand on your heart and affirm, "*This is my time, and I am ready for the next step.*"

Later in this book, I'll explain how this little mantra has changed the lives of literally tens of thousands of women. It reprograms you to believe that the Universe is looking after you, and that everything will be fine. Do this every day for a month, and you'll be astounded at what the Universe brings you.

Some chapters, on the other hand, will fire you up. When something moves or inspires you, take action on that thought *straight away*. Any success story you read in this book can happen to you, too. Share every piece of random luck with supportive people in your life. Even finding a small coin in the street is reason to celebrate!

The truth is that we're all capable of becoming unbelievably lucky. It's possible simply to choose to become a Lucky Bee, and to see the doors of opportunity opening automatically for you.

As I was writing this, I decided to take a music break to stretch and get re-energized. The famous Barbra Streisand song "How Lucky Can You Get" was the first song that came up on my playlist... I wasn't even aware of the awesome synchronicity of choosing this song as I started dancing around my living room. I just love any excuse to pretend I'm a Vegas showgirl.

As the song finished, I realized it was all about gratitude, abundance, luck, and loving life. Isn't that freaking *fabulous*? It was another message from the Universe that luck is ours for the taking. Luck is literally at our fingertips, just waiting for us to claim it.

I get messages like this all the time, and I always express my thanks for how I'm taken care of by the Universe. The fact is that we all are, all the time. We just need to be reminded every once in a while.

This book is designed to give you everything you need to become more consciously aware of what you're attracting into your life. It's intended to help you direct your energy into becoming luckier in the areas that matter most to you – whether that's in love, money, business, relationships, or health.

And don't worry: there really *is* enough for everyone. Just because you become a luck magnet doesn't mean that someone else in your life will have to go without. Nor will my supreme luckiness suck up all your good fortune. There's enough for *everyone* who wants it. We have an ocean of abundance, luck, and good fortune.

You can choose to be lucky or unlucky. Honestly, it's your choice; and you can consciously change your luck at any time.

The Universe doesn't distinguish or judge your desires: it just gives you exactly what you ask for. Chances are that you're already a good manifestor, so let's make sure you're using your powers for your highest good, shall we?

Let's get started!

Your first step is to download your action guide at www. DeniseDT.com/bonus, which will automatically make you part of our global Lucky Bee community. Plus, I'll send you some cool bonuses to keep you on the lucky manifestation train, and I'll be right here every step of the way, cheering you on.

How lucky can **you** *get?* Isn't it time you found out? I'm so excited for you, you Lucky Bee!

Xx Denise
Denise Duffield-Thomas
Money Mindset Mentor and Queen Lucky Bee
www.DeniseDT.com

Chapter 1

How I Became a "Lucky Bitch"

*H*ave you ever seen those crazy travel competitions advertised in the back of magazines and wondered, *Who actually wins those?* Personally, I'd just assumed they were a scam. Certainly nobody I'd ever met had won anything bigger than the meat raffle at the local bingo hall.

At least, I didn't believe it until it happened to me.

I want to share the whole story of how I won a luxury travel competition and became a professional honeymoon tester, because it really is a crazy story. I go into a lot of detail about the whole thing because I want you to look for the secrets hidden in my actions. It was a classic case of the Law of Attraction in action, even though I'd never experienced anything so magical before in my life!

Here's the short version of the story. In 2010, my husband Mark and I won a social media competition with a wedding company called *Runaway Bride and Groom*. The prize involved traveling around the world for six months for free, and reviewing the most exclusive wedding and honeymoon destinations all over the globe. All our expenses were taken care of, plus we also got paid a salary. Awesome, right? *Do you hate me yet?*

As part of our prize, we traveled to twelve different countries over six months, staying in some of the most luxurious hotels in the world for free. From tropical islands to sleeping under the stars in the desert, every day was something new. We went from our crappy little apartment to living in luxurious resorts with private butlers and fully stocked, complimentary mini-bars (and the fluffiest "rich person" towels; that was my favorite part).

We experienced the trip of a lifetime; and in return, we just had to write reviews of each place, write a monthly newspaper column, and make promotional videos of each destination. It was a dream job that tens of thousands of people around the world applied for; but as I'll explain, there was nothing "lucky" about the fact that we won. Since sharing the secrets of the win, thousands of other women have taken my practical tips to make magic happen in their own lives, too.

I promise I'm going to break what we did down for you; but first, a little bit of my background. This is really important to share first to give you some context.

I've been obsessed with personal development ever since I was fourteen. It started when I walked into a second-hand book shop and found an old-fashioned little book called *The Magic of Believing*, by Claude M. Bristol.

The book explained how you could deliberately create your own reality with your conscious intentions, thoughts, and feelings. Like many self-help books of that era, it was written for dudes, mainly to help them succeed at work. However, it was the first time I realized that I could change my destiny by tweaking my language and self-talk.

This was mind-blowing news to me.

I grew up in a small beach town, raised by a single mother and surrounded by people who didn't talk about stuff like that, let alone dream of a bigger life. I was even considered a bit of a freak because I loved reading so much generally, let alone being interested in topics like goal setting or Neuro-linguistic Programming (NLP).

I didn't have many role models challenging me to grow and to be a better person or to dream of a life for myself beyond that town. Oprah was really the only influence in my life who told me that circumstances didn't matter. She taught me that people can achieve anything they want, and I wanted to be rich and successful.

When I met her years later and got to thank her in person, I told her that she was the one who taught me to "break the cycle."

So finding that book at that impressionable age, when I first read about goal setting and the power of positivity, planted a seed that would germinate many years later.

I was the first person in my family to go to university; and my desire to improve myself increased even more when I moved to the "big city" and realized there was more to the world than I thought.

I joined a student business club (the international organization AIESEC) to surround myself with other motivated students. I spent my waitressing money on personal development seminars like Tony Robbins' *Unleash the Power Within* weekend, where you walk on hot coals surrounded by hundreds of people shouting and pumping their fists. I came out of those seminars extremely fired up, but with no idea of how to direct that enthusiasm into anything practical.

That was the story of my life at that point! Enthusiastic, but clueless!

I also read hundreds of motivational books, going through the classics like *Think and Grow Rich*, by Napoleon Hill, and *Rich Dad, Poor Dad*, by Robert Kiyosaki. These books kept me positive, but they didn't really change anything for the better in my life. I got good jobs here and there in my twenties, but then regularly sabotaged my career so I never progressed very far. That meant I didn't earn much money, despite being smart and motivated. (I also had *huge* money blocks, but I didn't know that then.)

I started businesses and entrepreneurial ventures, but I never made any money out of them, and my enthusiasm wore off quickly. I honestly felt like a failure – albeit a really well-read and positive one! Know the feeling?

I felt like all the personal development books and seminars weren't really changing my life in reality. *Think and grow rich?* I was thinking about money all the time – but it wasn't doing me any good! *Do what you love and the money will follow?* I wasn't sure *what* I loved doing or what my calling was. *Feel the fear and do it anyway?* I was plenty scared, but I wasn't sure what "it" was that I was supposed to be doing. Where's my sweet cash Universe?!

It was disappointing that my so-called "potential" wasn't going anywhere, and I went through bouts of depression because I thought there must be something wrong with me. I desperately wanted to prove to the world that I was worthy of living an exceptional life despite my humble background; but I was afraid the truth was that I was worse than ordinary. *I was mediocre.*

I even referred to myself jokingly as "Little Miss Slightly-Above-Average." Great self-talk there, right? When was it all going to fall into place for me the way the books promised?

When I first watched the Law of Attraction movie *The Secret* (based on the book of the same name by Rhonda Byrne), it really fired me up and renewed my passion to change my life for the better. I set an intention to find a mentor who could help me, and very quickly found Karen Knowler – a business coach based in the UK.

You know that quote, "*When the student is ready, the teacher will appear?*" Well, Karen came into my life when I was sick of my failed entrepreneurial efforts, and I'd literally said to the Universe, "It's my time and I'm ready for the next step."

See how powerful that small affirmation is? Karen's business course seemed perfect – exactly what I'd asked the Universe for – and I knew straight away that I wanted to work with her.

HAVE YOU SPECIFICALLY *TOLD* THE UNIVERSE THAT YOU'RE READY?

If you ask, and then a perfect opportunity presents itself, you *have* to say yes.

I listened to Karen speak about her program on a podcast, and I got this tingly feeling all over my body. Something was whispering, *"Yes. Do it!"* to me; and I immediately went out to get a bank loan to do her program. Now, I don't advise that you do the same – going into debt to do a program isn't always the best course of action, and I didn't make that decision lightly.

But I felt absolutely moved to take action, and something seemingly insignificant happened during that course that completely changed the direction of my life. One tiny but powerful exercise with Karen set into motion a series of events that led me from frustration and mediocrity to that five-star villa on the white beaches of Zanzibar.

DO YOU LISTEN TO NUDGES FROM THE UNIVERSE AND THEN *ACT* ON THEM?

On the first day of the course, Karen asked us to write down our version of our own ideal day. I'd never done this exercise before, and I can honestly say that it literally changed my life.

As you'll see from what followed, if I'd ignored or skipped that exercise, I *never* would have even found out about the travel competition, let alone won it.

So, if you do nothing else from this book, do this exercise: write down your ideal day in the most vivid detail you can imagine. And if you struggle with that kind of visualization, I've included a free guided "Ideal Day" meditation in the bonus section, along with your action guide. Before you read any further, make sure you go and download it now at www.DeniseDT.com/bonus.

It could change your life, too.

Now. There's a difference between knowing about a powerful tool and actually using it. During my time with Karen, she actually made us sit down and *do* the exercise – no excuses and no leaving the room (even though I wanted to… badly). Funny how we resist doing what we know what we should do, right?

I really laid my heart open during that exercise, and described a day so unlike my actual reality that I almost cried when I read it out loud to Karen and the other attendees.

Here's a summary of what I wrote:

Mark and I wake up in a beautiful king-sized bed with crisp linen sheets and an expensive mattress. The sun streams in the window and we can see and hear the ocean from our room. I wear relaxed and beautiful clothes. We go for a walk and swim together before we do yoga on our deck. We eat a fresh, luxurious breakfast, and then we go out exploring – or we can read on the beach all day. We have all the money we need to do the things we want to do.

We work from our laptops throughout the day, and I work on my writing; but our time is our own, and there is little stress. Every afternoon, we eat a gorgeous, healthy dinner together before watching the sun go down. Life is warm, sunny, relaxing, and abundant. We're both doing what we love, and life is just getting better each day.

When I read it out loud, it sounded ridiculous and incredibly unrealistic – I mean, *who lives like that?* (Um, I do now), but Karen, being very open-minded and a fantastic manifestor herself, was very encouraging. Even reading it out loud made it seem *slightly* more possible (but still virtually unattainable).

Here's how my actual life was at the time:

I reluctantly wake up early in a lumpy, bumpy double bed. I hate my alarm clock because it reminds me that I have to go to work. The slats on the bed are broken (despite my DIY fix), so we have to be careful when we get in and out of it, let alone anything more strenuous. The floor is absolutely freezing, but we have to skimp on heating because the bills are so high.

I head to the shower – sometimes the hot water works, sometimes it doesn't (it once broke for two months so we had "bucket showers").

I dress in my second-hand clothes, even though wearing corporate clothes makes me itch; and eat a quick microwaved porridge for breakfast. It's raining, so I make a dash for the bus, then take two trains to get to work. I clock-watch the whole day, head home in the dark, and finally eat dinner on my cat-pee-stained couch until I reluctantly go to bed.

Trust me, my life wasn't horrific by any means; but it was pretty far away from that sunny, chillpreneur life that I craved. And I had *no* idea of how to bridge the gap. Honestly, the only solution seemed to be to win the lottery!

I loved doing Karen's exercise, but when I left her seminar, I went straight back to my "reality" and my lumpy bed. I had an office job that I didn't love; and getting up to do my commute each day was a drag. I was unhealthy; and not only was I at least twenty pounds overweight, but I was also tired all the time. I was getting increasingly depressed about the crappy weather in London, and my financial situation was – frankly – crap, too. Mark and I were engaged to be married; and although our relationship was wonderful, I wouldn't say the rest of my life was a roaring success, despite all the books I'd read.

On the outside, I probably looked like I was a very positive person. On the inside, though, I often felt like a total loser.

I didn't know what to do, but – remembering how good it made me feel – I printed out my simple Ideal Day statement, and reread it every day. I even went one step further, and before I went to bed, I visualized myself going through that day. I could almost *feel* the sun on my face, even though in reality I was freezing my buns off.

I had no clue about how to make that ideal day happen, but reading and imagining it made me feel better.

✧ *Action* ✧

Write down your ideal day *now*.

I didn't have any sort of privileged upbringing. I had no special knowledge. I had a mediocre job, and a nice-but-mediocre life. But I also had a burning desire for more. I dreamed of more, and this was enough to kick-start my manifesting mojo.

Little did I know how powerful this one exercise would be, and how it would send me all over the world and completely change my life.

The journey was both easier and harder than I ever expected. Let me explain everything....

Chapter 2

How I Became a
Professional Honeymoon Tester

*B*efore I spill all the beans on exactly *how* I manifested our competition win, let me paint you a picture of the trip.

We started in New York, visiting famous landmarks like the Waldorf Astoria and the Empire State Building. Next we went to Kenya for two wildlife safaris in luxury tents, meeting real-life Maasai warriors, and seeing elephants and lions in the wild. *Incredible.*

After that, we stayed in expensive private villas on the sandy, white beaches of Mauritius and Zanzibar (where each night's accommodation could have bought us a small second-hand car). Then we…

❖ scoped out beautiful Catholic churches and wedding hotels in sunny Malta

- visited posh polo schools and beach-side horse camps in Spain

- camped out in the desert in Jordan as part of a horse and camel tour, as well as taking a tour of every five-star hotel in Aqaba

- spent weeks driving around the winding green highways of Ireland

- were treated to luxury yoga and detox retreats in Indonesia and Thailand

- finally topped it all off in beautiful Queensland, Australia (my home country).

It was *unbelievable* experiencing the world like that, in pure luxury. And it all happened for a reason (just not the most obvious one – don't worry, I'll explain).

The trip was not only a great experience, but something that changed my life in many ways. Most people would absolutely kill for the chance to do something like that, and I believe that I deliberately and consciously manifested it. I also believe that you can learn a lot of lessons from exactly *how* we did it.

There are many juicy details about how we won that competition that I've never shared publicly – at least until now. And those details really illustrate how "good luck" and hard work can combine to attract absolutely anything you want in life.

Can I tell you how I won it? Trust me, it has absolutely nothing to do with mere luck! I'd love to deconstruct what we did to show you exactly what's possible when you put your mind to it.

Make your own luck, then anchor it in

> *"Luck has nothing to do with it, because*
> *I have spent countless hours on the court*
> *working for my one moment in time,*
> *not knowing when it would come."*
>
> SERENA WILLIAMS

So was my winning this competition a fluke? *100 percent no.* I completely and *consciously* manifested the opportunity to travel around the world into my life. I used the Law of Attraction techniques I'm going to share with you to first attract the competition, and then to actually *win it.*

★ *Lesson* ★

You can manifest opportunities,
but you also have to take an extra
step with courage to claim them.

Remember that "perfect day" I described in the previous chapter? Well, a few months after I attended Karen Knowler's seminar, Mark and I got married; and our honeymoon in Asia was *exactly* like I described in my "perfect day." We got up with the sun shining, did yoga together, and explored new places all day long. We read piles of books; and ate fresh, exotic food. Those were three of the most beautiful and relaxing weeks of my life as we traveled around Singapore, Indonesia, and Australia.

I kept that ideal day vision in my head as we planned every detail of our honeymoon, and I imagined what it would be like to have it come true.

And then actually living that life, even just for three weeks, was enough for me to believe that my day-to-day reality could be equally as wonderful. It also made me determined to experience even more of it.

For example, on a tiny island in Indonesia, we stayed in a rustic cabin that was built on stilts right into the ocean. It only had one bedroom and a bathroom; but after the grayness of our life in London, it felt as relaxing as a five-star hotel to us.

One evening, it was beautifully balmy and we could see millions of stars above us.

I stood on our deck, facing the dark ocean, almost in tears at this amazing experience; and I said aloud, "Universe, I want more of this in my life. This is what I want. Please show me a way I can create this for my life every day. I'm ready for more."

I stood on my tiptoes with my arms stretched out to the Universe, and then put my hands on my heart and imagined roots growing out of the bottom of my feet to anchor that experience deep into the earth. I wanted to remember that feeling forever, and come back to it when I needed to, especially after we went back to our cold, dreary life and our sad little apartment.

Our honeymoon was incredible, and we lived my ideal day for three weeks straight… But eventually it ended, and we had to go back to "reality."

I dreaded going back, but after experiencing what was possible, I knew I had to focus on what I wanted, and not on what I *didn't want.*

For the next six months I remembered the feeling of standing on that wooden verandah in Indonesia, under the beautiful night sky, and *knowing* that it was going to happen again. Every day on my commute, while I was standing under an umbrella in the rain or eating lunch on my break, I mentally went back there: using that anchor I'd created to re-experience that evening through my imagination.

I'd feel the warm night breeze on my bare, tanned skin (even though I was really wearing three layers of itchy, second-hand clothes). I'd feel the anticipation of doing something adventurous that day after eating exotic fruit for breakfast (even though I was at work, eating microwaved soup). And, in short, I focused *every* cell in my body on what I wanted.

✧ *Action* ✧

Anchor every positive
experience to attract more.

Bring it into your present reality, any way you can!

What I wanted was travel, warmth, freedom, abundance, and adventure. So, I started telling everybody who'd listen that Mark and I were going traveling again. I just repeated it as if it were fact: *We're going to go traveling for six months next year. I'm really excited about it. It's going to be amazing.*

And our friends would ask, "Where you are going to go? How are you going to afford that?"

"I don't know yet. We'll figure it out."

And of course, that's *exactly* what we did. Little did we know what the Universe had in store for us. We didn't need to know all the answers. Our job was to dream it, and get closer to believing it every day.

★ *Lesson* ★

Confidently talk about your dream as if it's already a reality.

As I was brainwashing myself to believe that my dream was happening, I automatically started thinking of ways I could make it possible. Maybe I'd write an e-book or start an online business, and earn enough to take six months off work. Perhaps we could travel to conferences for free if we did some speaking or helping out behind the scenes. I was willing to get creative.

I set very specific goals, wrote them on some Post-its, and stuck them on my wall at home, including:

- six months of travel with Mark
- staying in places for free somehow
- £3,000 a month spending money (around $US4,000).

I had no idea what it would really cost, but I knew I had to get specific around the goal. I figured that number would be just what we'd need to go traveling and backpacking around Asia.

✧ *Action* ✧

Write down your goals – be as specific as possible.

Those goals on my wall kept me sane, because I knew I couldn't live trapped and miserable anymore. I was desperate for freedom and adventure; and instead of feeling stuck in my current circumstances, I could channel all of my frustrations into experiencing that vision in Indonesia over and over again.

On a practical level, I had a few business ideas in my head, but I wasn't that attached to anything in particular. All I could think about was getting to go traveling: remembering the warm breeze on my skin, and seeing the beautiful stars. That vision kept me going through the cold London winter.

Something interesting happened next: two very close friends got made redundant from their jobs, and while they were *thrilled*, I was immediately crushed. (Note – don't be surprised when your goals start manifesting for other people in your life!)

When you're made redundant from a job you hate, and you're in your twenties, it's *freaking awesome*.

One friend got a six-month payout, and the other got eighteen months' tax-free salary!

I'd like to say I was happy for my friends, but when I heard the news, I was completely insane with jealousy. I *hated* going to work every day; and suddenly my friends were not only liberated from their corporate jobs, but they could also both afford to go traveling (which is exactly what they did). It was so unfair! That was *my goal*!

If I'd been made redundant, I would have packed up my stuff in ten minutes flat, booked my trip, and probably started a business, too!

Instead, I was bitter about their luck, and asked myself "Why can't someone pay *me* to go off and decide what I want to do with my life? Where's my lucky break, mofo?!"

However, I knew this resentment wasn't going to get me anywhere, and was a total waste of manifesting energy. So despite feeling like a two-year-old who wanted to throw a tantrum, I decided to acknowledge my jealousy, and my new affirmation became:

"GOOD THINGS ARE HAPPENING FOR ME, TOO. MY LUCKY BREAK IS JUST AROUND THE CORNER."

That affirmation made me feel *marginally* better (even though the jealousy stayed just under the surface, threatening to boil over at any time). After all, it's natural to compare yourself with others, or feel like someone else's win comes at your loss. Still, I decided to wish my friends the best and feel happy for them because I knew that I deserved good things, too. My lucky break *was* just around the corner!

I had to believe that, and every time I noticed myself getting jealous, I tried to immediately replace that feeling with anticipation and hope. I'm not saying it's easy, but every thought counts, so you have to be extremely vigilant about your energy.

Then, in the New Year that followed, I got a text completely out of the blue from my friend, Christina. In it was a single sentence that completely changed my life. It said, "I've found your perfect job," with a link to a travel competition website run by *Runaway Bride and Groom*. And honestly, the second I saw the text, I knew that it was divinely guided. I'd never seen or heard anything about that competition anywhere else – just that one shot. Somehow, fate intervened and got my attention. I think I still owe you a cocktail, right, Christina?

I can still remember the competition write-up…

Wanted: Honeymoon Guinea Pigs for the Ultimate Job in the World

One lucky couple will travel to some of Runaway Bride and Groom's *fantastic destination wedding and honeymoon locations around the globe, testing hammocks for their relaxation qualities, champagne for its bubbles, and honeymoon suites and locations for their romantic allure! Apply here…*

Then, in the fine print: "*Six months of all-expenses-paid travel around the world for two people.*" The gig was writing hotel reviews, and the salary...? You know what I'm going to say, right? It was £3,000 per month. I'm not even kidding. It was exactly what I'd asked the Universe for, exactly per the Post-it on my wall.

The second I looked at the website, I said to myself, *This is **exactly** how we're going traveling.* I just knew it from day one, no doubt in my mind. From that second, nobody else on the entire *planet* had a chance at winning that competition.

But remember – this part is important. If I hadn't already told *everyone* I knew about my goal of traveling around the world with Mark, chances are that I wouldn't have found out about the competition at all. If I hadn't spent hours convincing myself that it was going to happen, my friends might not have believed me. Maybe Christina never would have thought about me when she saw that website. The opportunity might have passed me by completely.

So it wasn't by "chance" that I "happened" to find out about the competition. Looking out for opportunities like this was layered into my subconscious the moment I started mapping out my "ideal day." Abraham Hicks calls this "rockets of desire": a way to send your request out to the Universe.

I added weight to my rocket by reinforcing the goal and having visible reminders everywhere (i.e. the Post-it notes on my wall). I anchored the goal into my reality by experiencing it in the real world on my honeymoon – and I enrolled other people into my belief by sharing my desire with my friends. A lot of behind-the-scenes, deliberate action went into that "chance" text from my friend.

How many chances are you missing by keeping your goals to yourself?

✦ *Action* ✦

Tell your (positive) friends
about your wildest dreams.

Next: do the work – make it happen

Mark came home that night to hear me babbling incoherently about the competition; and I flat-out told him we were going to win it. That was how we were going to go traveling – it was a done deal, dude!

And this insanely awesome man saw the determination in my eyes; and, bless his heart, he responded with, "Okay, let's do it."

He'd played along with my goal setting and talk of traveling for months; and now he got swept up in my enthusiasm and utter conviction. He didn't say, "That's ridiculous, why would we win it?" He just jumped into the dream with me.

We put together an application video immediately (it was due by midnight), but I swear we almost got divorced doing it. It was a complete disaster. Lucky the judges never saw *that*, because we were hardly the best role models for teamwork that day!

The task was simple. To apply for the competition, we had to make an eighty-second video about why we were the best couple. Sounds easy, right?

But we couldn't agree on our script, and I yelled at him because he wasn't getting it right, then he yelled back at me for being too picky.

We dressed up in fancy clothes, but we didn't have a camera – so we filmed it on my old Nokia phone against a plain wall. After a few takes, I realized that Mark wasn't looking into the right lens so he looked cross-eyed. I was pissed and frustrated that it wasn't going more smoothly. After all, wasn't this *the* opportunity? Why wasn't the Universe helping?

Have you ever noticed that even when a great opportunity comes up – one that you *know* is right – the Universe seems to conspire against you? Or maybe the resistance hits, and you procrastinate so much that you figure it's just "not meant to be?"

Luckily, we persisted. Mark had to learn video editing from scratch, with me criticizing it over his shoulder. It really was a terrible video in hindsight, but we looked friendly; and during it, we showed a bunch of pictures from our own honeymoon. You'd never guess that in between takes, we were yelling at each other and barely talking by the end of the night. I wanted it so bad, and I was angry at myself that I seemed to be sabotaging the opportunity before we even got started.

We almost gave up several times that night, because it seemed too hard. That's the tragedy. So many people would have seen that exact same competition and *not* put in an application because they found it frustrating or technically difficult. They would have thought, *So many people are going to apply. Why would we win anyway? There's no point doing this.* They might have given up at the first hurdle. I wonder how many half-finished videos for that competition are out there?

I've missed important deadlines for speaking applications or awards for the exact same reason before. Once I felt a little resistance, I rationalized that it probably wasn't "meant to be" and gave up.

But because I had months of conviction from my goal setting, I knew I had to break through that resistance. I decided to see our challenges as just a little test from the Universe – to see if we *really* wanted to win the competition. We got through that night barely on speaking terms, but we got our video in five minutes before the deadline. Many didn't. I'm sure that 80 percent of people who *intended* to apply gave up, forgot, or self-sabotaged it in some way.

We know now that more than 2 million people visited the competition website each day, but in the end, only a fraction of them entered. Plus, a surprising number of couples didn't read the instructions properly, so their entries were ineligible because their video went over time or they missed something simple off their written entry. But this opportunity was so important to me that you bet I read *every single detail* of the competition criteria, and made sure we met them.

★ *Lesson* ★

Be persistent through hurdles
- there's less competition
than you think.

Get in and get it done!

Something else happened that was completely in our favor. Even though we got our video in on time (just), the judges decided to extend the deadline by a week because they were suddenly attracting worldwide media attention, and their website couldn't cope with the number of entries.

I learnt this one important lesson purely by accident: *Be one of the first to apply.* Because we hit the original deadline, our entry was number 183. By a complete fluke, and for the first time in my life, I handed in something early. I've always been a last-minute girl, and I could have missed the deadline, too, if I'd had a last-minute panic like normal. The Universe *was* helping us!

Why is this important? Remember that competition judges (and potential clients) are people, too. Behind the competition were three real-life humans – Rosemary Meleady, Jillian Godsil, and Zara Stassin – each with experience in travel, PR, and wedding planning. They were all super-women, but they still only had twenty-four hours in their days.

So the first couple of hundred videos were exciting for them, and they watched their favorites several times. But soon, they were being interviewed about the competition on TV and radio stations all around the world; and the interest in the competition exploded globally.

In the last hour of the new deadline, thousands of entries came in *every minute.* The competition coordinators enlisted their entire staff to watch videos non-stop for days. But those latecomer videos had to be pretty memorable to compete with the early entries. By complete "luck," ours had been one of the early ones.

That's my biggest advice for you if you're applying for a business award, or even a competition like *Survivor* or *The Amazing Race*: be one of the first to apply. It's a universal truth that most people wait until the last minute. To stand out, make a memorable video, and get in front of the judges while they still have functioning eyeballs. And use the same principle if you're applying for a grant or a writing competition, or sending in a proposal for your dream client.

✧ *Action* ✧

Find out the deadline and
put it in your calendar *now*.
Then get it done *early*.

Throw everything at it

From the moment Mark and I sent the video to the judges, we'd already won in our own minds. We were going traveling. Yay!

But of course, there was more to winning than that. We didn't just put in our video application and get chosen randomly out of a hat. The selection process took months. How did we actually do it? Once we put in our application, we did absolutely *everything* we could think of. We put every technique that I'd ever read in any personal development book into practice, because I didn't want to leave anything to chance.

I'm going to share all of the tips we used with you in this book, so you realize that there's *always* more for you to do. There are millions of subtleties involved behind the scenes of any "lucky break."

That said, I think the biggest secret behind winning the competition was that we kept our eye on the prize. We never, ever, ever gave up believing that it was a gift from the Universe. We *knew* that this opportunity was ours, and we didn't let any doubt or fear sabotage us... but we weren't overly attached to it to the point of desperation. I thought it was an amazing opportunity that had come into my life for a reason, and I was going to go for it with everything I had. However, it was the *traveling* that I wanted, and that I focused on. This is a crucial point in successful manifesting – think *beyond* the *how*.

One of the most popular early articles on my website is *Can You Win the Lottery Using the Law of Attraction?* I wrote it because I was sick of getting emails from people who said that their biggest (or only) goal was winning the lottery. It's a huge mistake to focus all your attention on something as arbitrary as winning the lottery, and block any other way that the Universe has to bring you the abundance and lifestyle you want. Winning the lottery isn't the only way you can create an amazing life.

If you think, *But Denise, one of my goals **is** to win the lottery*, I'm going to challenge you to focus on what you'd do with the money. Do you want to win because you want a huge mansion or a beach house? Do you want to go traveling around the world? Maybe you want to give money away to charities? Focus on that end goal, not on exactly *how* the money's going to come to you. I'm serious. Winning the lottery isn't a goal – it's what you'd *do* with your winnings – that's your real goal.

I could never have imagined that I'd win a competition against tens of thousands of other people; and that *that* was how I'd manifest my around-the-world travel dreams. My end goal might have come in another way entirely. The Universe is infinitely more creative than we are.

Beyond that, pay attention as I tell you all the little things I did to win the competition. There were many practical and metaphysical actions that kept my vibrations high and focused on the outcome.

In fact, I started recording my actions and tips when we were about halfway through the trip. I knew they'd make a fabulous book; and I knew I wanted to share what I'd done with as many women as possible afterward. (Oh, and by the way, before I found out about the competition, I was asking the Universe to send me a great book idea).

I couldn't sleep one night while we were staying at a retreat in Bali. So, after tossing and turning for hours, I got up in the middle of the night, took my diary into the bathroom, and wrote down every tiny little thing I'd done up to that point. What I wrote then formed the basis of *Lucky Bitch*, the book you're reading right now. This stuff works, and what you read will make it easy for you to manifest *your* wildest dreams, too.

★ Lesson ★

There's a bigger reason
behind your dream.

Harness the power of your unconscious mind

*"Visualize this thing that you want, see
it, feel it, believe in it. Make your mental
blue print, and begin to build."*

Robert Collier

My biggest manifesting tip is to use the power of your unconscious mind through creative visualization. You've heard this a million times before, but do you commit to doing it daily? It really is so powerful; and you're only limited by your creative imagination. You have to watch your thoughts constantly, because a negative visualization works just as powerfully as a positive one. Without meaning to, you can often imagine the worst happening (especially if you're creative), so make sure you use that power for your highest good instead.

Let me give you an example. How often do you "rehearse failure" by imagining the worst, or feeling bad about an outcome before it's even happened?

I have. I've spent nights sleepless at 3 a.m., worrying about things not working out, or obsessing about the past and what I've done wrong. This is a total waste of your manifesting energy.

Once Mark and I had our application video in for the competition, we spent hours each day visualizing ourselves traveling through airports, on the plane, looking out of the window, and feeling excited about the next adventure. In my mind, I was already lying in a hammock with a cocktail in hand. The vision was comically at odds with my then-reality – living in an awful apartment with mismatched wallpaper in every room, and commuting every day through the gray winter. It took every ounce of my imagination to overcome the dissatisfaction I felt with my life.

But that's what it takes. Turn your thoughts to what you *want*, despite the reality of your situation.

Mark and I created a shared visualization where we actually won the competition, rehearsing that moment when the judges called our names. Our anchor words to each other were, *"Mark and Denise!"* As in *"The winners are... Mark and Denise!"*

All day long, we texted each other words of encouragement. When we came home from work, we greeted each other with, *"Mark and Denise! Mark and Denise!"* We visualized ourselves telling people about winning, saying, "Oh, my God, you're never going to guess what happened. We won the competition!"

It was the perfect shorthand to snap us back into positive vibes.

Before we went to sleep at night, we spoke about how awesome the trip would be, waking up with the sun streaming through our bedroom, doing early morning yoga, and re-creating our wonderful honeymoon together. I'd go to sleep dreaming of it all coming true. It was the last thing I thought of at night, and the first thought each morning.

And I have to say, I probably wasn't the best employee at this time, because all I could think about was traveling. *I was obsessed.*

So, get really honest with yourself. Are you absolutely obsessed every moment with your dreams coming true? Are your thoughts consumed with those dreams, or are you allowing doubt to creep in?

You don't have to do it forever. I don't keep that level of obsession up every single day. Some goals are more important and urgent than others. But if you want to move FAST to manifest the things you want, make it a priority to visualize all day long.

✧ Action ✧

Visualize your success.

Get your feelings on board

Every Law of Attraction book I've ever read tells you that *thinking* is not enough to manifest what you want. You have to *feel* it. You have to get into that space of living it before it actually shows up in the real world. Every cell of your being has to be convinced.

You'll probably have to fake it at first to overcome all the evidence that's in front of you. This is where I get emails from people saying, "But Denise – I can't ignore

the reality. It's really true that I have *no money right now.*"
Maybe, but how is focusing on that helping you to change
the situation?

Being able to *feel it before you see it* will massively
improve your manifesting ability, because the Universe can
only give you more of what you already are. Feel rich and
abundant, and you'll believe that it's possible. That way,
when opportunity shows up, you'll be more inclined to act
in the way a rich and abundant person would.

Of course, that can be hard in reality. I'm not saying it's
not. But again, what's the alternative… you don't achieve
your dreams? You rely on a long-shot lottery win?

I have a little trick I use that works like a charm to excite
my entire body with the prospect of my dreams coming
true. And you can use it, too.

You know that little flutter of excitement you get in
your tummy when something awesome is happening? It's
almost the same feeling as fear, or as when you're in love.

You can fake that feeling, and your body won't know
the difference. Try it now. Feel the twinge of excitement
deep in your belly, even if you feel like you're just flexing
your tummy muscles. Say out loud, "OMG, I'm so excited!"

This simple exercise also activates your sacral chakra,
which governs your feelings and sexuality, i.e. your ability
to receive pleasure and enjoy your life.

I knew I had to increase my capacity for pleasure
in order to receive the massive opportunity that the
competition brought, and believe that I deserved to win
it. Activating the twinge of excitement and anticipation in
my belly helped me to believe that winning was possible.

My physical body might have been sitting at my desk or on the train looking out at the gray winter sky; but in my imagination, I was miles away, lying on a beach with the sun on my body… and I allowed myself to get excited about it. I consciously manipulated my emotions to pretend it had already happened. I got myself into that space *every single day*. Did it make a difference? You bet!

This exercise also helped me when we had to take some scary action that was well out of our comfort zone to win the competition. I told you it wasn't just an arbitrary win: we had to convince the judges over several months that we were the right people for the job. And every minute I spent rehearsing our success made me more confident about its inevitability.

How would it feel to achieve your biggest goal? Exciting, ecstatic, relaxing? How would you feel if you knew it was a done deal? Practice that feeling now, no matter how unrealistic it seems.

★ *Lesson* ★

Feel it to believe it and
bring it to life.

Another technique you can use to create this feeling is called "afformations" (not a typo). The author Noah St. John wrote a fantastic book called *The Little Book of Afformations*, which introduces the concept of phrasing affirmations in the form of a question.

Instead of saying your affirmation as a statement like, "I am happy and healthy," you change it to a question like, "Why am I so happy and healthy?" There's a different energy around afformations because when you say them, you activate that part of your brain that likes to solve problems. I wrote my afformations out regularly, with questions like:

⟡ *"Why am I so lucky?"*

⟡ *"Why am I about to go off on a great adventure?"*

⟡ *"Why are we the best people for the Honeymoon Testers' job?"*

Try this technique out now. When you do, notice that it has a really interesting frisson to it. That's because the phrasing implies that the possibility you're writing about is already a reality, and it gets you excited about the outcome.

Funny update on this: I actually hung out with Noah and his lovely wife Babette a few years later in an amazing resort in the Dominican Republic. I told him how his book helped and inspired me to create my Lucky Bitch empire, and he was thrilled!

✧ *Action* ✧

Turbocharge your affirmations
- try afformations!

Connect to the bigger picture

Another key shift for me was having a greater purpose for winning the competition. I never thought, *Well, wouldn't it be nice to have a free holiday?* Instead, I was thinking, *This is going to change my life. I'm going to tell so many people about how I won by using the Law of Attraction; and it's going to change their lives as well. This is going to have a ripple effect throughout the Universe.*

I had a big reason behind what I wanted that was greater than me. That made it hugely emotional, and the highly charged emotions told the Universe I was serious.

I remember one day I was standing at the train station in my winter coat, and rehearsing the speech I would give at conferences after we won the competition. That image took my mind off the cold, and sent energetic threads out into the Universe, pulling my future toward me. The other commuters must have thought I was crazy as I paced up and down the far end of the train platform, speaking aloud to myself. I didn't care then, and I *still* practice like this today. When I'm driving somewhere, I'll often rehearse a future speech, like an interview with Oprah or a TED Talk.

Your words are powerful, and speaking your vision aloud helps you see a bigger picture beyond just achieving your goal.

I knew that winning the competition was aligned to a greater purpose for me that went way beyond the thrill of the free six months of travel.

The seed had been planted much earlier than I thought. I'd asked the Universe for business ideas and book ideas years before we'd even started talking about traveling, so I imagined that the Universe had big plans for me.

I knew the competition was an amazing opportunity that I could leverage for the rest of my life – into books, speeches, and courses. It was *proof* of the concepts I'd been talking about for so many years. I daydreamed about launching my career as an author, a speaker, and an entrepreneur; and this opportunity fit in nicely.

I was so certain I was going to win that I was practicing the speech about how I'd manifested it, *before* I'd even won it. In fact, I knew I was going to write *this very book*, before we won the competition.

Do you get what I'm saying?

★ Lesson ★

Think beyond the *how* and pull
your dreams toward you.

In short, I was convinced that winning the competition had a much higher purpose for me. The travel was just the icing on the cake.

Additionally, rehearsing the speeches I would give in the future helped me to detach from winning the competition, because it was just a stepping stone – not the end goal in itself. Sound delusional? Well, sometimes the pure self-belief you need to manifest your desires into the real world almost *has* to border on self-delusion!

I constantly told all my friends, *"We're going to win it."* When we got into the top fifty, I said, "We're going to win it." And then, when we were in the top ten couples, I said, "We're going to win it." I repeated this so often that my friends started to believe me, too, which increased my belief even more. Belief is infectious!

> *"When you believe in a thing,*
> *believe in it all the way, implicitly*
> *and unquestionably."*
> WALT DISNEY

★ Lesson ★

Pay attention to *why* you want it.

When people tell me they want to win a car competition or a major raffle prize, I ask them, *"Do you want the new car, or do you want to win the competition?"* Because, if you *really* want the outcome, then you don't care HOW you achieve it. You might just pay for a new car. You might start working toward your dream house. And trust me, the Universe might have something unexpected in store for you.

Use real-world, practical tools to tune the Universe to your goal

Now, let's get practical. I promised to give you extremely easy and doable tips in this book; and there's something you can do to start manifesting your dreams straight away.

Get out your diary.

As soon as I found out about the competition, I scheduled it in my calendar. I blocked the entire six months out with "Honeymoon Testers." *Why?* Because scheduling it made it real. It was a commitment.

This is a really important practical *and* metaphysical technique. If there's something that you really want to go to – a conference, a holiday, or whatever – *schedule it.* When you do this, you're energetically making space and telling the Universe that you're ready.

I was asked, "Denise, are you going to go to that conference next year?" I'd say, "Actually, we're going to be traveling then, so no." I was being honest because I knew that I was going traveling no matter what. And I was serious about it. Each time I said it aloud, I believed it a little more.

There was no "If we win..." I spoke about it as if it were a done deal.

On a practical note, blocking it into my calendar also made me declutter my schedule, so I could actually *go* on the trip when we won it. (Notice I said "when" and not "if" there – I was extremely vigilant around the language I used when I spoke about the competition.)

As soon as I scheduled the trip, I saw that we were going to have to miss a friend's wedding. I accepted that, and then went one step further by officially declining her invitation. I figured that if we didn't win, she might be okay with squeezing us in, but I was prepared to miss it either way. Does that seem rude? Well, if you're hesitating around making a firm commitment, then maybe you don't really believe that it's going to happen.

Most people would do it the other way around; *if* they won, then they'd decline. But I didn't want any energetic clutter, so I took care of declining as a show of faith.

I also got used to the idea that we'd be away for our first wedding anniversary and my birthday. No big deal. I had to make sure I had no distractions and no energetic blockages to moving forward.

What's holding you back? Fear of pissing people off? Worried about your dreams not coming true? Are you really ready for what you're telling the Universe you want?

✧ *Action* ✧

Do it. Make energetic space. Put something in your calendar *now*.

Scheduling the trip made it real, but it also made me look at other practical considerations. We'd have to rent out our apartment while we were away, find sitters for our cats, and budget really carefully to make sure we could still pay our credit card bills and mortgage while we were away. The salary involved would cover some expenses, but most of it was paid as a bonus toward the end. (Another practical consideration – find out *all* of the details so you have no nasty surprises later.)

We knew there'd be a lot of logistics for us to sort out, and figured, "*why leave it all to the last minute?*" If we really believed that we were going to win, why not take care of it all straight away?

Taking action like this serves two purposes: it shows absolute faith *and* removes any obstacles in your way.

The first manifesting step I always teach people now is to declutter their lives of every kind of distraction: mental, emotional, and physical. Who knows? I could have energetically blocked the whole opportunity because I was unconsciously worrying about how to pay our mortgage while we were away, or how to break the news that we couldn't make our friend's wedding.

The Universe doesn't want to create unnecessary stress for you. So if you don't clear the obstacles first, your goal might not end up being in your highest good, and might cause unforeseen problems. Clear the decks to avoid this.

Here's how this worked for us: just a few weeks after submitting our video (and scheduling the travel into our calendar), we got the news. The judges had selected fifty couples to go into the next round, and we were on that list. The morning that they announced it, I actually dreamed that we'd been selected – I was literally thinking about it night and day. We woke up to the news that we'd made it, which didn't come as any surprise to either of us. We both just felt so aligned to the opportunity that all we had to do was to get into the right space to receive it.

You can't declutter enough in pursuit of your dreams. We started to pack up our house in preparation as if we were going traveling (because, after all, we were!) We culled our possessions, packed extra stuff into our attic, and made lists of what we'd need to live in tropical climates.

When in doubt, declutter. I've done this every time I wanted to move house, too – whether I was selling or buying. The first thing I do is start packing!

✧ *Action* ✧

Get rid of the distractions
and look after the practical
considerations. Let the
Universe know you're ready!

Simple rituals with big results

But wait! We did more!

Obviously our job still wasn't over at that point. We'd been short-listed into the top fifty, but we were still a long way from winning. What else could we do to show the Universe that we were really serious? The answer is "every single manifestation technique I could think of!" I was seriously leaving *nothing* to chance for the opportunity of a lifetime.

Dream boards

I made a travel dream board with pictures of all the places I wanted to visit. I made it my desktop picture on my computer, both at home and work, so every time I turned on my computer I saw it. It was just another anchor to make me think, *The winners are... Mark and Denise!*

Dream boards are a powerful anchor to your dreams, and they don't have to be fancy. I often use Pinterest now as my online dream board, but I still usually download my fave picture to my phone, laptop, and desktop, so I can always see it at random times of the day.

✧ *Action* ✧

Dream boards *work* –
create one today!

Passwords

Have you noticed that most of my tips are simple reminders of your goals? Here's another one that works so well, I still use it today.

I changed my work password to "HoneymoonTesters," so I had to type it out at least ten times a day. Every time I did, it gave me a little jolt, and a reminder to affirm, "*Yes, I'm going to win this!*"

It will only take you a couple of minutes to change your password, but doing so will create magic in your life. This is especially important if you're still in a day job, because anything you can do to remind yourself of your goal is going to help. Your new password can be related to your new income goal, for example "6figures" or a specific goal like "newhouse."

Make your phone work for you

Your phone can be a good manifesting tool, too. I already mentioned that I put a photo on my phone's lock-screen, but I also changed Mark's name in my mobile phone to "Mark – Honeymoon Tester Buddy." Every time he called me, I'd be reminded to affirm again, "*Yes, this is going to happen!"* I put daily pop-up reminders into my calendar so a message that said, *"Congratulations on winning the Honeymoon Testers' competition!"* would pop up at random times.

See how simple but powerful these anchors are? Plus, you don't have to think about them. I don't know about you, but I don't have the time or patience to meditate for hours each day on my goals (plus I'm super-lazy)! That's why I like unconscious reminders.

And every time you remind yourself of your goals, you will get to that powerful place of *feeling* the win. Type, draw, visualize, doodle, think, and feel it constantly. There are unlimited possibilities.

Make sure you download the free action guide that comes with this book so you can check off every manifesting tip. That will make sure you're giving yourself the best chance of achieving your goals.

Use a circuit breaker

Because I did these little rituals, I didn't have time to let doubt or fear enter my thoughts. I had many reminders about what it would feel like, not only to win the competition, but also to go traveling. There was no room for doubt.

Okay, that's a small lie. Occasionally, there was a little voice that asked, *But… what if you **don't** win?* I'm serious when I say I told that voice to "Fuck off!" to break the association, and then I'd shake myself physically to get rid of it. I wore an elastic band on my wrist, and would snap it if I found myself thinking negative thoughts (and I sometimes do this today, too). It takes practice to stay positive.

Remember the Ideal Day exercise? That wasn't a one-off thing. I used my journal every day to write it out again, but with more specific details about the Honeymoon Testers' competition and winning it. I also wrote down repetitive mantras like, *"I am the Honeymoon Testers' winner." "I won the Honeymoon Testers' competition." "How exciting that I won this Honeymoon Testers' competition!"* It was a process of constant reinforcement. Sounds boring? Well – really want an extraordinary life? This is what it takes.

Sometimes I did my "dream journaling" before I went to sleep. Other times I did it during my commute to work. I even did it during boring work meetings, so I looked super-productive!

★ Lesson ★

Getting obsessed with your goal
every waking moment works. Every
little reminder and anchor helps.

I don't want you to think that all we did was visualize and write a few words in my journal, and then – Ta-daa – we won the competition. The work wasn't purely metaphysical. However, the excitement behind the dream gave us the courage to take action in the real world. I believed it was possible and inevitable, so I acted accordingly.

Get out of your comfort zone and give it all you've got

Nothing will really ever happen if you just sit around and wish for it. You know that; and the personal development industry often does people a great disservice by pretending that results are effortless. Manifesting takes time and commitment – and honestly, most people don't have the persistence to do it for a day, let alone the weeks, months, or even *years* it takes some goals to manifest.

Mark and I knew that it wasn't enough to just dream. We had to get far out of our comfort zones to prove to the judges and the Universe that we wanted to win. So, we cold-called newspapers and radio stations to generate our own press and PR. That was scary. Our local paper covered the competition and wished us luck. A local radio station interviewed us.

We contacted celebrities, and got people like Tim Ferriss and gossip blogger Lainey Lui to tweet out support for us. A little tip on this – I noticed that Tim was always on social media really late at night, so I messaged him at 3 a.m. when he would probably be less distracted from requests.

Mark used his contacts in sport to get famous footballers to hold up signs saying, "*Mark and Denise are the Honeymoon Testers.*" At one of his work events, there was a Queen Elizabeth impersonator who gladly held our sign for a photo. We tweeted out, "*Even the Queen supports us,*" and tagged the judges. We wanted to make sure that we were regularly getting *their* attention, too, so we spaced out these PR wins.

I'd been building a big online network for years after going to conferences around the world, and I asked people to comment on and share our videos. Many people obliged happily.

★ *Lesson* ★

You may as well ask, because you never know who'll say yes!

Another time, the PR consultant for Tourism Queensland just happened to be in town speaking at a conference. The year before, Tourism Queensland had created the "Best Job in the World" competition for a blogger to live in tropical Queensland for a year. So I knew the consultant would be likely to have some good tips about what the judges were looking for, and the coincidence that she happened to be in town was too good to ignore. I had to follow the nudges of the Universe.

Speaking to strangers is something that really stresses me out; but after the consultant's speech, I went and asked her for advice. She said, "Be yourself and *be prepared*." Then we took a photo together, and I tweeted it out, tagging the judges.

She also introduced me to the winner of her Queensland competition, Ben Southall, who also tweeted his support. Why did I do all these things? I wanted to show the judges – and the Universe – that I was willing to go the extra mile.

✧ *Action* ✧

Build your network before you need it.

I knew that the ability to generate buzz was one of the things that the judges were looking for when they created the top fifty short list. My background in marketing and social media really paid off, but this time there was more at stake. So I did things I'd never had the confidence to do before. I cold-called a newspaper editor who was so bitchy to me on the phone that I squirmed in embarrassment. But I didn't care, and kept going. I knew that we could outwork *anyone* if we just tried hard enough. Some of the other contestants were doing press, too, but it was pretty hard to beat the network Mark and I had been building for years.

It's easy to think that sitting around and lighting an abundance candle is enough manifesting effort, but honestly, there is *always* more you can do. Get creative and get hustling.

★ *Lesson* ★

You'll succeed if you do the work - most people won't.

The next stage of the competition involved selecting ten couples to compete in the final judging panel in Ireland. We didn't want to take any chances, so leading up to the announcement, we spent time making additional YouTube videos to make sure the judges knew who we were. We just knew that we'd be there at the final. And (spoiler alert!) we were.

When the judges called to tell us personally that we'd made it into the Top Ten, we were thrilled to see that we were getting closer and closer to our dreams. The Universe was just saying, "Yes, yes, yes."

But again, we had no time to rest. We knew we had to take it one step further. Remember, there's always *more* you can do. When people tell me they've tried "everything" in pursuit of their dreams, I know that usually means, "I tried one or two things, and then I gave up and hoped for the best!"

We wanted to make sure that we were *the* most prepared couple in the final. Destiny is one thing, but being prepared is always as important. When destiny comes knocking, you don't want to be caught slacking in your underwear, do you?

The Roman philosopher Seneca once said that luck is, "*what happens when preparation meets opportunity.*" How prepared are you willing to be?

We thought, *Okay, it's going to be a whole weekend of challenges with nine other couples. What could they possibly get us to do?*

Then we brainstormed *everything*. We thought they might test us on geography or random facts about Ireland. We researched everything, just like you would for any job interview. For example, we studied all of the honeymoon and wedding destinations that Runaway Bride & Groom had covered in Ireland and abroad. We made sure that we were prepared and ready. And believe me, we were.

We went walking every morning together before work, and during the walk we'd quiz each other.

We'd rehearse potential questions the judges could ask us, "Why do you want to win this competition? Why do you think you're the best couple? What are each other's strengths and weaknesses?" We prepared it all. We were total geeks, but we really wanted to win, so we wanted to be more prepared than anyone else. Not only that, but waiting for the results was painful, so we needed to stay positive and not "psych ourselves out."

★ *Lesson* ★

There's no substitute for being prepared.

How can you show that you're really serious?

The next thing we did was to ask ourselves what else could stand in our way. And here's where we decided to do something quite drastic.

One of the potential downsides to winning the competition was finding tenants for our apartment, which we couldn't afford to leave empty for six months. Well... finding them wouldn't necessarily be a downside, but it *would* be a hassle if we waited until we knew we'd won, because there were only ten days between the winner announcement and the first day of the trip.

Being short-listed in the Top Ten meant we were one step closer to winning, but I didn't want any energetic complications. And we were so convinced that we were going to win that I decluttered the problem by advertising the apartment for rent before we went to the competition finale. We prepared a tenancy contract, then prepared the house for potential tenants (we decided to rent it as furnished).

We paid for extra advertising on rental websites, interviewed people, and set an intention to find the right tenants. It paid off, and days before we left for the final panel, we found two students who wanted to rent the apartment for six months. Perfect.

This is where you might be thinking, *Denise, why would you do that when you weren't 100 percent guaranteed you were going to win? Isn't that unethical?*

Even though we had no Plan B, I knew I wanted to change my life so badly that I was willing to move anyway, even if we didn't win the competition. Read that again – *I was going traveling* **anyway**.

I was willing to do what it took to get out of that place because I didn't like it any more. There was no risk; there was no downside to taking that massive action, and the payoff was that it took another potentially stressful situation off my to-do list. To be on the safe side, the weekend before we left for the Honeymoon Testers' final, we had the students come over to sign the contract and give us their rental deposit.

I said to them, "Look, we're going away for the weekend, so I'm not going to bank this deposit until we get back on Monday. But in the meantime, the apartment is yours, and here's the contract." I just knew, regardless, that we were going to move.

✧ *Action* ✧

Take steps to show you're *really* serious about your goals.

You think that was bold? The next action was terrifying but necessary. As soon as we found out that we were in the final, we told both our bosses at work. Can you imagine? "Um, so we're in the running for this global travel blogging competition, and we're pretty sure we're going to win it."

We had very mixed reactions to the news.

Mark's boss said, "Wow, cool. Great opportunity. Of course, you have to go for it." I don't think his employers quite believed that he was going to win. So it wasn't a big deal for them.

But my boss was not at all supportive, and kind of pissed about it. She made me hand in my resignation there on the spot, and then basically didn't talk to me until I left. It created a stressful situation for my final few weeks, but I had to be single-minded and keep my vibrations positive.

She told me that she wouldn't be able to give me a good reference, to which my first thought was, *I will never have to apply for a job again after this*. And you know what? That was my last ever job. I knew it was THE opportunity that would change everything for me.

I'm not telling you to quit your job; but for me, I knew that I'd inevitably leave anyway. You have to gauge your own capacity for risk. Personally, I was *all in*.

★ Lesson ★

Not everyone's going to be very
supportive of your dreams. You
might get some backlash. Screw 'em.

It was an emotional time, cutting so many ties to our life; so it was really important to keep my eye on the prize as much as possible. Hence all of those little anchors I mentioned earlier. When my boss gave me the cold shoulder, I just looked at my dream board hidden in my desk drawer and thought, *And the winners are... Mark and Denise!*

Speaking of anchors, here's one more tip that's really easy: wearable affirmations, like jewelry, temporary tattoos, and even clothing.

I had a lucky necklace – a pretty silver medallion with the word "*Yes*" on it – that I wore every day. It was another reminder that, "*Yes, I go for opportunities,*" and, "*Yes, this job is going to be mine.*" Every time I felt unsure about my decisions, I looked at my necklace and smiled. Each day at work where I could feel the resentment simmering off my boss, I touched my necklace and mentally thought, *And the winners are... Mark and Denise!*

Do you see how important it is to constantly surround yourself with positivity? Nothing is too small or unimportant.

Every activity compounds, and who knows which action will make the ultimate difference.

✧ *Action* ✧

Throw everything at it, no matter
how wacky or woo-woo it sounds.

Use everything, especially the super-woo tips!

Now, the practical stuff is essential, but I love me some woo-woo manifesting tips, too!

The movie *What the Bleep Do We Know?* talks about alternate Universes, and the theory that every possibility exists simultaneously at any one time. *Sliding Doors* also has the same kind of theme. The theory in both movies goes that there could be different versions of you out there that chose different things in life.

Somewhere out there is a version of you who decided to become a professional dancer, or rock star, or activist, etc. There are so many different ways that your life *could* have turned out. Both quantum physics and quantum mechanics say that all of those possibilities exist somewhere out there in parallel Universes all at the same time, which is kind of wacky and crazy.

However, I decided to use that theory to fire up my creative imagination and make my dreams even more attractive to the Universe. I thought, *Somewhere in the Universe, I have already won this competition. It's inevitable that I've won it. It may be a remote probability, but in one particular Universe, it has already happened. So all I have to do is find that Universe and consciously jump into it.*

Remember how Mary Poppins jumps into the chalk drawing on the sidewalk, and she goes into a completely different reality? That's what I wanted to do: choose the reality in which I win the competition.

Sounds insane? I don't care. *Throw everything at it.*

I shared this idea with Mark, and I'm so happy that he was open-minded! Can you imagine how wacky it sounded? On our morning walk, I'd say, "There's a Universe in which we've already won this competition. It's a mathematical certainty. Let's find that Universe." And we'd pretend to jump into it together.

It sounds totally crazy, but these daily rituals made me feel even more certain that we were going to win the competition. They compounded my belief, and helped to me make scary decisions in the real world, like telling my boss that I was quitting my job, renting out the apartment, and mentally preparing myself for what was to come.

★ *Lesson* ★

Be willing to be a little
"freaky" if it gets you
closer to your dreams!

Be ready to be tested

A week before the final, something happened that was completely out of our control. Again, I chose to see it as a test – as the Universe, asking, "*Are you willing to keep the faith when things seem hopeless?*"

The hiccup for us was called Eyjafjallajökull, (the Icelandic ash volcano), which erupted and canceled flights all around Europe *for weeks*. It seemed like we weren't going to make it – was the Universe against us? But, after some initial fears, we decided that we were prepared to swim to Ireland if we had to. We started researching overnight trains, ferry options, and even private charters.

I told Mark not to worry: we'd get there fine... and we did! The ash cloud cleared just in time, and the Duffield-Thomases were on their way!

We arrived in Kinsale, a gorgeous seaside town in Ireland; and planned out our strategy for the final judging events. Everything we did was going to convince the judges that we were the right couple for the job. This wasn't a free weekend jaunt: we were in "work mode."

First, we went to the tourism office and got a map to familiarize ourselves with the town, which definitely came in handy later on. Remember that cheesy saying, "Prior Planning Prevents Piss-Poor Performance?" That was our motto. Luckily, Mark had been a boy scout in his youth so the map seemed important, and we spent the hours before the "Get to Know You" event studying the whole town – just in case we'd need it.

We checked into our hotel (apparently Michael Jackson had stayed in our room while visiting Kinsale a few years before), had showers to refresh ourselves, and rehearsed our "surprised" faces for a few rounds of, "*And the winners are... Mark and Denise!*"

We walked confidently into the first event, and immediately introduced ourselves to the judges with, "Hi, we're Mark and Denise!" Even the way we said this was deliberate. Rather than saying, "My name is..." we said it like we assumed they already knew who we were.

Without being arrogant about it, we wanted to show supreme confidence that we were winners.

Then there was our competition to size up. We knew there were nine other couples to beat, but we didn't know much about them. One couple had come from the USA, one from Canada, two from the UK, five were Irish, and there was one South African/Brazilian couple.

We didn't watch any of our competitors' videos, and I didn't learn much about them before the weekend. That sounds arrogant, but I didn't want to psych myself out. I knew my only real competition would be allowing doubt, fear, or anxiety to creep in.

I see a lot of entrepreneurs pay so much attention to their competitors that they second-guess themselves. I've now found that blinkers are the best. Stay in your own lane, and use all of your manifesting energy for your own goals.

We had people come up to us and go, "*Ah, you're Mark and Denise! Oh, I love your videos.*" And I would be thinking, *I don't know who you are.* I just wanted to focus completely on us, and make sure that we made the best

impression on the judges. That doesn't mean we were
unfriendly – but it does mean we remembered that we
were there for *one* job.

★ Lesson ★

There is no competition. You
can only be yourself.

Be prepared for every challenge

The final weekend played out like the Amazing Race, but
luckily without the reality TV cameras. Because, seriously,
there were times when Mark and I yelled at each other
under the stress (never in front of the judges, though!)

We didn't know what to expect, but we guessed the
judges would want to see professionalism, creativity, and
positivity. We also made a pact not to drink too much of the
complimentary champagne, which *also* came in handy later!

Mark and I gathered together with the other couples
as a group to receive our first task: there were eight secret
dinner reservations at different restaurants in town. The
two couples who didn't find a restaurant had to eat at
the local fish and chip shop, while everyone else got free
dinner at a fancy restaurant, and had to produce a written
review by the next morning.

We were dismissed to our rooms for about an hour
before the mini-bus van came to pick us up. We looked at
each other, and then leapt into our game plan.

We got out our map from the tourism board, and got on Google Maps. We looked at every restaurant in that town and marked their names on our map. Then we jumped on the bus into town, psyching ourselves up the whole way.

I know for a fact that not every couple did this. Some couples hung around chatting and drinking the free champagne, refreshed their makeup, and got ready for a free night out with fun people. We didn't. We prepared, because we knew that however light-hearted the tasks were, it was game on – and the Duffield-Thomases were here to win. No excuses. Play hard or go home.

What happened that weekend is the perfect example of the Lucky Bitch philosophy. There's always unseen preparation and planning behind almost any success story. We might have seemed like we'd had many lucky breaks that weekend, but nobody prepared more than we did. That's why we won.

✦ *Action* ✦

Do everything you can think of to guarantee your success.

We got into the town, and were given cryptic clues to the different restaurants. It must have been hilarious for the locals seeing ten couples literally running through their small town. Both Mark and I had running shoes on (prior preparation prevents piss-poor performance, remember!), but some of the women had high heels on because they thought they'd be going out for a nice, free dinner. We easily found one of the hidden restaurants using our map, and checked it off as a success.

How lucky, right? No luck – just preparation and teamwork.

As we started our appetizers, we saw one of the other couples arriving sweaty and stressed at the restaurant, only to be turned away. One couple saw everyone running right at the start, and decided they wouldn't win the challenge anyway – so they went straight to the fish and chip shop! Why did they even bother coming?

The dinner was awesome, but we were in work mode: taking notes and photos of the menu for our restaurant review. Luckily, we hadn't drunk much free champagne – we had to work for several hours that night writing our restaurant review. Then, first thing the next morning, we sent it to the judges, and immediately started preparing ourselves for the next challenge.

Round one: Team Duffield-Thomas!

The map and the running shoes seemed like a good idea, especially when there was a similar treasure hunt challenge the next day to find a hidden radio crew. The first couple that made it to the judge got a live interview.

Mark and I knew that winning this would be an awesome way to promote ourselves, and to show what we could do in front of a camera. We looked at each other and said, "We're going to win this!" We made sure that we had our map handy, and worked together as a team... so it was inevitable that we were the first couple there. We knew we were starting to make an impression when the second couple turned up and said, "Ugh, the Duffield-Thomases!"

Damn right.

It wasn't like we were super-competitive and horrible to everyone else. It's just that we knew it was our big opportunity, and we weren't going to leave anything to chance. Other couples were fitter than us (the running-around time was pretty painful for me), but we outsmarted them with superior preparation.

The biggest challenge of all was to make two videos throughout the weekend, which – honestly – was a new skill for us. One was a promotional video about the town, and the other was about the Honeymoon Testers and why we were the best couple for the job.

We'd figured right from the outset that making videos would be a major part of the competition, so we'd actually started working on ours already, which meant we didn't have to start from scratch. We'd been practicing using video editing software, and we had little clips of our own wedding and honeymoon ready to go. We'd also figured that any video about being honeymoon testers would need a bit of "wedding flavor." Plus, we'd created a folder on our computer of pictures of Ireland, and the town; and just in case, all of the logos for *Runaway Bride & Groom* and the competition sponsors. And our photos were already cropped to the right size.

As we ran about the town doing the other challenges, we also started filming "b-roll" footage, and drafted a script. Then, at night, we'd upload that into our video editing software to save us time. We even had some royalty-free background music ready to go!

This was, in hindsight, quite a smart thing to do. Making those videos was stressful, and there's no way we could have done it last minute – it was another potential divorce moment!

✧ *Action* ✧

Brainstorm every
potential "problem" and
solve it beforehand!

Making those videos was tough – I'm not going to lie. Several of the other couples were professional video editors, or had amazing cameras – so we knew we couldn't compete on skill set alone. Our passion and attention to detail, however, was going to help us immensely.

Over the next two days, we used every free moment (and there weren't many) to work on those videos. We even took our laptop on the mini-bus into town. We had to have incredible teamwork, taking turns recording voice-overs and editing until four in the morning.

So was it easy? No. We were exhausted after running around town and smiling enthusiastically. Free champagne was on offer, and it would have been way more fun to let our hair down and party with the rest of the couples. The reality was that it was incredibly stressful; but we didn't want to make it this far and then lose on a technicality like not getting an assignment in on time, or missing out an important instruction. We'd seen how many couples were eliminated in the first round because their application videos were just two seconds too long.

Of course there were some last-minute hurdles. Spotty Internet in the hotel meant that all the couples were freaking out about uploading their final videos. Luckily, we'd finished our ones hours before the deadline. Submitting them early meant that the judges probably had more time to watch them before the final announcement. Trust me, being early is not usually my style, but this whole experience really taught me the value of not just being on time, but being *early*. After all, the early bird gets the worm, right?!

✧ Action ✧

Read the instructions, and just do the freaking work!

Of course, we didn't want to be hermits who just hid in our room, working the whole time. We also wanted to make sure that the judges saw us as reliable people, willing to go that extra mile: cheerful, and ready to undertake the next challenges in front of us. So we always made sure we were on time for every single meetup, lunch, and challenge; and always offered to help out. We took turns working and networking. And we always, *always* had smiles on our faces!

We wanted to subtly brainwash the judges with our happy faces, so that they started rooting for us. This isn't a Law of Attraction technique, it's a life thing. If you've read the classic book *How to Win Friends and Influence*

People, you'll know it breaks down those interpersonal skills that make people want to help you. Tiny tweaks in your personality can make you seem like a lucky person.

Being agreeable, pleasant, nice, and approachable were all important to us, because we wanted the judges to see that we could represent their brand and their competition better than anyone else.

So far so good.

The last hurdle was the final job interview with a panel of four judges. We'd rehearsed so much that we knew who was going to say what before we went in, plus we had some creative marketing ideas ready to go. We'd prepared little signals to each other about how we were going to answer different questions, too. So if there was a question on a tough topic for me (like geography), Mark would cover it without us looking at each other in confusion.

★ *Cheesy Lesson* ★
Teamwork makes the dream work.

Convince yourself, convince everyone else

With me wearing my "Yes" necklace, we went in the interview room and told the judges that we knew how important the competition was to their brand, and that we wanted to be a part of their team. Straight up, we pitched them on the Duffield-Thomases.

We didn't want to be arrogant or overwhelm them with our preparation. Instead, our focus was to make sure the judges knew that we wanted to win, and that we were up for it. We went in with a new killer creative idea, too: if we won, we could renew our vows in every country and break a Guinness World Record for "Most Married Couple." (We had *no idea* that the current record at the time was eighty-three weddings! That's a whole other book.)

This definitely got their attention, because we were bringing something new to the table. But beyond that, we went all out on convincing them that we were the people for the job… without being annoying about it. We believed that we were going to win, and we could see that they were starting to get swept up in our belief, too.

★ Lesson ★

Conviction is contagious.
If you don't believe it,
why would anyone else?

Then it was result time. After three days of busting our butts on crazy challenges, it was time for the final reckoning. Was it all going to pay off? Or were we going to have to go back to our life, tell our friends that we didn't win, disappoint our potential tenants, and beg for our jobs back?

No. We were exhausted and frazzled, but we needed to pull together our last dregs of self-belief. No time for doubt.

The moment arrived, and all the couples lined up in front of the assembled press, judges, and competition sponsors. Knowing that the winning couple would have to do immediate interviews, we were already wearing fancy evening clothes. We were ready. There was nothing else we could do; there were no more practical or energetic hurdles to overcome. We were literally packed and ready to go traveling for six months.

As we sat there waiting for the result, Mark and I whispered to each other, "*Mark and Denise. Mark and Denise. Mark and Denise.*"

Seconds before they announced the winners, I leaned over to whisper to Mark, "*You thank the judges. I'll thank the venue.*" We never once considered that we wouldn't be called as the winners.

✧ Action ✧

Keep your belief right up until the last second.

Who *knows* what the other couples were thinking at that moment? They might have been stressing out about how to break the news to their boss, or what they were going to do with their apartment and pets... We actually found out that one of the couples had just been offered a new job and was conflicted about it. Were they packed and ready to go, or did they just figure they'd cross that bridge when they came to it? That's how most people operate, right? *"Universe, send it to me, and I'll figure it out later."*

We were energetically ready though. There were no emotional obstacles in our way to keep us from receiving this opportunity. I squeezed Mark's hand as I imagined one last jump into the magical chalk drawing.

And sure enough, they announced the winners, saying – wait for it – "And the winners are… Mark and Denise!"

Mark and I looked at each other with excitement but little surprise. We were already *there* mentally and emotionally. We were literally ready to go! Our house was decluttered, we had tenants to move in, our resignation letters were already handed in – nothing was standing in our way.

The Universe (and the judges) just caught up with our desire. Everything got swept up in our goal.

Abraham Hicks talks about unmet desires being held in "vibrational escrow." This means that what you want is being held somewhere for you, just waiting for that opportunity to be given to you. We already felt like travel was in our vibrational escrow. It just happened to come from this particular opportunity.

The Universe was paying up!

Be cool with not everyone being happy for you

We were thrilled and excited. Our friends and family were equally ecstatic. However, in the time it took to change for the celebration dinner, some people had already written negative comments online. They were clearly really pissed off that their friends and family hadn't won. It was our first taste of negative press and being criticized. Ouch.

The public at large, having of course wanted *their* loved ones to win, were not happy with the outcome. So they took their frustration out online, saying really horrible things about us: that we were boring and didn't deserve to win; and even that we were cheaters.

One person found out about our apartment advertisement, and said, "Well, this is rigged because they obviously knew they were going to win."

One of my friends, Angela, actually responded to the online criticism with, *"No, she was just manifesting it and visualizing!"* which just made me laugh so much. My friends understood what we'd achieved, but to the outside world it seemed like pure luck.

★ *Lesson* ★

Not everyone will be happy about your success.

This lesson can be hard to deal with. Success does come with a certain amount of criticism, and many women hold themselves back because that idea is so unbearable to them.

Are you asking, "Universe – send me success but with absolutely *no* downsides. I want a big business with no unhappy customers ever. I want to create a big network, but I never want anyone to unsubscribe from my newsletter ever. I want to be on Oprah, but I'd die if someone wrote me a hate letter?"

You're asking for the impossible.

What you have to realize is that the criticism isn't really about you. After all, how many times have you made a comment, online or off, like, "Look how fugly that dress is," or had a point of view about a total stranger's marriage? You sometimes just do it without thinking about the real person behind your comment. Put yourself in that situation. The same thing is going to happen to you. People won't think that you're a real person.

You know what they say about opinions and butts? Everyone has one!

The criticism didn't put a dampener on our win at all. We recognized it for what it was, and it didn't bring down our high. We actually laughed – we were about to go on an all-expenses paid trip all around the world. *Lucky bitching!*

Only two couples out of the nine actually said anything to us after the win. It was an awkward gala dinner with at least seven couples who were so angry and disappointed that they could barely see straight. One or two couples made fools of themselves. One couple actually yelled at one of the judges in the bathroom. Another couple just left the hotel straight away, not even grateful for the experience. I mean they didn't win, but they could dine out on the story of the final for years! It was a crazy-fun experience.

★ *Lesson* ★

Nobody likes a sore loser.

Those couples all shot themselves in the foot with their bad attitudes. What if we got sick and couldn't fulfill our duties? They were never going to be called up in that case, were they?

Know you'll get your goal, no matter how it happens

Winning was inevitable for us because we were in the right "Universe" to win. But if we hadn't won, we would have said, "Hmm, that sucks. I wonder how else we're going to go traveling, because this is happening regardless."

Some of the other couples were just certain they were going to win on the surface, but perhaps they didn't have everything in alignment. Some were so attached to the outcome of winning that they were completely devastated when they lost. As I mentioned earlier, we weren't necessarily attached to the idea of winning – we were attached to the idea of *traveling*. If we'd lost, we would have thought, *Cool. If it didn't happen, we're still going traveling somehow. Let's make that happen now.*

I see a lot of people get totally bummed out when things don't work out the way they want. *"Bummer, I didn't win the lottery last night. Well, I guess I can't buy that house now!"* How important is the dream to you? Are you willing to do what it takes to find another solution?

★ Lesson ★

Don't give up on your dream if
one possibility shuts down.

One of the couples actually wrote online, "We can't believe Mark and Denise won. They were the least charismatic of all the couples." Nice.

We were focused on what was important: winning the challenges and charming the people who mattered. Impressing the other candidates didn't factor high on our scale of importance, because it didn't affect the outcome. The judges had to know that we could do what they needed, not whether we could win a popularity contest with people who had no influence on the outcome.

✦ Action ✦

Focus on the important
details, forget the rest.

So after the final, we packed up, went home, and got ready for our new adventure. Winning the competition was cool, but I knew this was going to have far-reaching ripples throughout the Universe. And it did.

Little did I know that during the next few years, everything that I'd imagined would come to fruition. I wrote two more books (this one and the best-selling

Get Rich, Lucky Bitch!), and got my life coaching certification. I became a well-known Law of Attraction speaker and money mindset mentor to women all around the world. I gave the speech that I'd rehearsed on that cold train platform many times in real life. And guess what? I've never needed to apply for another job ever again in my life. All thanks to those Post-its (and a million other actions along the way!)

What happens when you manifest your goal?

So that was how we won the Honeymoon Testers' competition and manifested our goal of six months of traveling around the world.

How was it? Well, it was an incredible, *life-changing* experience.

It was hard work, but it was 100 percent worth it. Together, Mark and I visited twelve countries, wrote more than two hundred posts on our travel blog, wrote seven Irish Times columns, filmed and edited one hundred and thirty videos, and did more than a hundred media interviews, including live TV. And we did all this in our first year of marriage.

It was fun, stressful, and above all, *extraordinary*. The judges even took us up on our offer of renewing our vows in every country, so we got married eighty-seven times around the world. Yep. I don't even like weddings! But it was a small price to pay for the experience.

It also opened my eyes to a new world of luxury and abundance, and gave me a glimpse of how rich people vacation and live their lives. It let me experience that ideal day of freedom and adventure over and over again. I honestly think that was the bigger picture that eventually led me to become a money mentor. I needed to stretch my capacity for wealth and pleasure; and trust me, nothing says "luxury" like having a private butler take care of your every need!

We eventually did exceed the Guinness World Record of the time of eighty-three weddings. Of course, by the time our application was processed, the current record holders were up to ninety-nine weddings, and I was totally over it by then. I was ready to move on to my next adventure – starting my business as a mentor, speaker, and author.

So yeah, I'm unofficially the *second* most married woman in the world, and I'm happy enough with that. I'm going to write more about the trip one day, and I think it would make a fantastic screenplay (who would play me? Drew Barrymore or Kate Hudson?). Mark and I got married in so many unusual ways: with a Maasai tribe in Kenya, surrounded by sharks and stingrays on the Great Barrier Reef, on lighthouses and in castles in Ireland, in a minus 120-degree cryotherapy room, and many more. The Honeymoon Testers' judges had a great time coming up with weird and wacky ways for us to get married. Trust me, it would be a hilarious movie.

Weddings aside, one of the most useful lessons from the trip was how much *work* went on behind the scenes. The daily blogging deadline and recording videos formed the skill set I still use today in my business.

What can *you* do to manifest your dreams today?

So. Cool story. But how does it apply to *you*?

Why did I share so many in-depth details of this story? I've repeated it so many times, I'm almost sick of it myself; but I wanted to show you how much commitment you need toward your dreams. How every little thing compounds and builds upon your belief. How constantly applying the Law of Attraction principles can move physical reality and bring any dream to you.

This is what it really takes.

✧ *Action* ✧

Ask yourself, "What can
I apply from this story?
What's possible for me?"

Look at the biggest goals in your own life and ask yourself if they're what you really want, or just what you think *can* happen.

Can you dream bigger? Are you really committed to making what you want happen *no matter what*?

I know you are.

Is there more you can do to manifest your dreams?

I know there is.

If I told you I won a global travel competition without any further details, you might think, *Wow, she's so lucky!* But now that you know the behind-the-scenes story, do you really think that it was luck?

This is an unbelievable story of a dream that I manifested out of thin air. Do you know how many times I've heard, "Oh, you lucky bitch! I'm so jealous."

But it wasn't random, was it? Look at all the daily actions I took to win the competition. There was actual, measurable work that went into winning it. I didn't just write down "travel" as a random New Year's resolution and then have it magically come true without any effort. I worked on that goal for nine months before the competition opportunity showed up. Then it took two months of intense effort to actually win it. That's almost a year of daily obsession and commitment to a goal. How many people give up after a week? How many half-heartedly buy a lottery ticket and think that's enough.

It's not.

If one opportunity doesn't pan out, find another way.

If a door shuts, open a window.

If the window won't open, kick down the door.

Decide right now that you'll *never* give up.

It takes conscious effort to do those visualizations every day, and courage to do things that take you out of your comfort zone. It takes far more of both than you think.

But now you can take the practical lessons behind this story to manifest amazing things for your own life. You can make the impossible real. The rest of this book is full of even more practical examples of how to manifest big goals into your life. We'll go through specific examples – not to win competitions, but to apply the same principles to manifest common goals like love, good health, more money, and business opportunities.

We're really going to get *real* about what it takes.

But never forget that the Universe will help you with even the biggest goal – in far more creative ways than you can think of yourself.

> *"I used to think – there must be thousands of girls sitting alone like me, dreaming of becoming a movie star. But I'm not going to worry about them. I'm dreaming the hardest."*
>
> MARILYN MONROE

When you believe that your success is inevitable, all you have to do is walk toward it. Your dream is already seeking *you* out, too, so start moving toward it. This book will tell you exactly how.

Harness the luck that's available for you, grab those opportunities, and most of all – do the work. You can be one of the ones who people say, "You're such a lucky bitch!" to.

And when they do, you can just smile and reply, "I know. And good things are happening to you, too."

Chapter 3

The Ten Lucky Bitch Commandments

You want to know exactly how I've become a luck magnet? Don't worry, in this chapter I'm going to spell it out *completely* for you, so that you can join the thousands (one day millions) of other Lucky Bees around the world and embrace outrageous success for yourself.

Here are the ten steps I used to get where I am now:

1. Start with forgiveness
2. Get over yourself
3. Be grateful
4. Treat yourself like a VIP
5. Get your boobs on board
6. Some people will think you suck: get over it
7. Good is good enough

8. Create your own karma
9. Manifesting is a muscle
10. Luck is an inside game

Every technique I share with you works in different ways, and you'll probably have to try more than one. Try all ten, and your chances of success will go up exponentially! My philosophy is to throw *everything* you can at creating the life of your dreams. Trust me: it's worth it. Something will work eventually; but because you're making an effort and telling the Universe what you want, the solution may appear in a completely different way from what you expect. It may even seem like magic – sometimes the Universe works in mysterious ways.

Wait – is this for real?

It's easy to get caught up in wondering *why* something you've tried works, rather than just being grateful for it and getting on with your manifesting. Some people might say that your results are due to the placebo effect. (You might even privately think this yourself!)

Is manifesting simply the placebo effect? Who gives a crap? Seriously, I mean it. I don't care if something works because of positive suggestion. I only care that it *works*. I don't pretend to know the exact reason these techniques work: I just know they've made a real and lasting practical difference in my life, and in the lives of tens of thousands of others in the *real world*.

Optimistic people expect good things to happen to them, and then those things happen. It's as simple as that.

What I teach here, and to the community of Lucky Bees around the world, is how you can consciously create those things for yourself.

1. Start with forgiveness

I'll talk about forgiveness until my tongue gives out and your ears fall off. Why? Because if I was only allowed one personal development tool in my superhero Lucky Bee utility belt, I'd choose forgiveness over and above everything else.

> *"Holding on to resentment is like drinking poison and expecting the other person to die."*
>
> UNKNOWN

Forgiveness is the reason that I've been able to move on from my past, break the cycle of dysfunction, and consciously create my present life. I've seen for myself the transformation it creates in my Lucky Bees' lives. It can literally transmute the energy of the Universe to work for you, instead of against you.

In my late teens and early twenties, I spent so much time in resentment and anger. I blamed my "crappy childhood" for why I was lost, why I couldn't be happy in a job, and why I attracted idiot boyfriends. It was *my parents'* fault that I was so messed up. If only they'd done a better job, I'd be stable, happy, and "normal." They really screwed up!

I even resented people who seemed light and happy. It made me sick to see how effortlessly they went through life, while I saw myself as "damaged." The contrast between them and me made me feel even worse, lucky bitches!

It's alright for them... I thought... *they had a perfect childhood.* How lucky they'd been to be born to middle-class parents who had money, didn't divorce, gave them everything they asked for, and helped them to become the lucky people they were! From the outside, that's what it looked like to me. Other people had perfect lives, and I didn't deserve one.

As humans, we can hold grudges that go back many years. I've heard from Lucky Bees in my Bootcamp who've held on to memories for more than forty years, but they still remember an event as if it had happened yesterday. It still upsets them to tears.

Those memories take up so much space and energy that they can kill your enjoyment of life like a noxious weed. They can poison your current relationships, and hold you back from experiencing love. Even when something good happens, there's an underlying sense of "*I don't deserve this*" or "*good times never last.*" You sabotage yourself to prove how messed up you are, or to prove that you're a terrible, unworthy person.

It's an easy pattern to fall into, but that blame, shame, resentment, and anger will block you from living the life of your dreams.

Are you ready to give up your resentments?

You can *choose* what you focus on. You can use that energy to live the life of your dreams, or you can endlessly relive the pain over and over again. Meanwhile, the person you're angry at is probably just living their life, oblivious to your pain.

It wasn't just my parents I was angry with. I'd lie awake at night, recounting a work conversation from years before, still feeling angry at my boss. The unfairness and the feeling of being taken advantage of still lived within me. It affected my sleep and my ability to move on, because I *still* kept attracting bosses and careers that treated me the exact same way. Do you relate?

I went to counseling several times, and just cried the whole time. I couldn't articulate everything I was angry about. I could easily recite my "story" – growing up with a young single mother, not much money, witnessing domestic violence, and my "less than ideal" childhood – but I couldn't believe there was a way out that could make me feel better about it. I wanted a magic pill.

My lingering resentment of my mother made me hate myself, because I looked and sounded just like her. I spent most of my twenties living in London, many miles away from my family in Australia because I was so... fucking... angry.

I was terrified of manifesting a serious illness from my anger, and I came close many times. In my twenties, I had many health scares: a suspected brain tumor that turned out to be nothing, hospitalization for pneumonia, and mysterious aches and pains. Not to mention how tired and lethargic I felt all the time.

One summer, I was so depressed that I said, "God, I wouldn't be upset if you ran me over with a bus." I didn't want to actively commit suicide, but I had no joy in my life and was apathetic about my future.

The light bulb moment for me came when I learnt about the power of forgiveness through Louise Hay and her beautiful book *You Can Heal Your Life*. Louise credits self-love and forgiveness as *the* most powerful gift you can give to yourself. I agree, and now that I've included forgiveness as a tool in *every* single one of my programs (yes, even my Money Bootcamp – forgiveness works for money, too), trust me when I say that it creates miracles in every area of your life.

Now that I've experienced it, I credit forgiveness as the single greatest thing I've done for myself. I don't regret the thousands I spent on personal development; but I wish I'd realized that everything else was just a Band-Aid until I went to the root of the problem and just *forgave* everything I saw as unforgivable.

I believe that all the self-help in the world is not enough if you don't practice forgiveness (and yes, I include self-forgiveness in this). Everything else in the personal development world is awesome – but it's just the icing on the cake. Forgiveness is the main dish.

Seriously – walking on hot coals with Tony Robbins was amazing; but once the buzz wore off, I was still just as angry and confused as ever. I needed to get to the true core, and forgiveness was the only thing that truly worked.

A true secret of outrageously successful women is the ability to transmute negative emotion into positive results. Reliving the hurts of the past takes up real energy that we can use instead to create, to love, to experience, and to deliberately manifest a truly vibrant life.

The best technique I've found for forgiveness consists of four simple phrases:

> I FORGIVE YOU...
> THANK YOU...
> I'M SORRY...
> I LOVE YOU...

This mantra is similar to the Hawaiian practice of Ho'oponopono: a ritual of reconciliation and forgiveness. (Often Ho'oponopono starts with "please forgive me," rather than the other way around).

Doing this simple forgiveness exercise will eliminate a massive proportion of your personal hang-ups, and make you feel lighter than ever before. The best part is that you don't even need to have a conversation with anyone to forgive them, so there's no need to physically stand in front of people or make an awkward phone call. You can forgive the deceased and people you've never met.

When you've done this, you'll be able to harness your own luck guilt-free. You'll be able to start consciously creating your ideal life, and even transform relationships in the real world *without* your baggage clouding your perception of reality. When you get rid of all the emotional crap that you've been carrying, your natural talents and love of life can shine through. You can go forth into a brighter future – happy, free, and unencumbered by your past.

Hear me: this is *not* about victim blaming. This is important to understand, especially if you're feeling resistance or even anger toward me for *suggesting* that you forgive terrible people in your life.

Forgiveness doesn't condone or justify bad behavior. Some people are absolute douchebag monsters – there's no doubt about it, and you may have experienced things that are honestly unforgiveable. However, what purpose does it serve for *you* to carry the pain of what happened to you forever? The person who hurt you has probably moved on with their life, so *forgiveness is a gift you give yourself, not them.*

Do you really get that? Forgiveness is for *you*.

Nothing is too large or small for you to forgive. And it works on everything.

For example, are you in debt right now? You can do forgiveness work on yourself for being in debt, forgiveness work on the debt itself, and forgiveness work on anyone you feel has contributed to you being in debt. Whether you blame the government, or your university, or the bank for lending you the money when you really shouldn't have borrowed it, forgive it all.

Or maybe someone *else* has gotten you into debt. It's really (unfortunately) common for women to go into debt to help others. Or maybe you didn't realize that someone was getting you into debt. Maybe your debt is from a divorce or marriage (otherwise known as "sexually transmitted debt"!). Forgive them, too. I talk about forgiveness in my money book *Get Rich, Lucky Bitch!* because it works just as well for your wealth, and it clears the decks for more abundance in your life.

What if something truly horrible happened to you?

First of all, I'm really sorry for your experience. There's nothing else I can say except, "*That sucks.*" And now? It's okay for you to release the burden, and allow yourself to move forward in happiness.

How do you do that? Forgiveness.

I've read amazing stories of people who've rediscovered joy in their life by forgiving their kidnapper, or forgiving the drug addict who killed a member of their family. Peace of mind, grace, new possibility, and healing were all gifts that they gave *themselves* when they forgave.

How do you actually do it? Do you need a special forgiveness kit? To buy a new course? Get a certification? Wait for Mercury Retrograde to be over?

Nope. You don't need any of these.

Instead, you can do forgiveness work through a simple but powerful ritual. There's no need to wait until a full moon, or get naked and light candles (although you can if you want). And it doesn't need to be perfect.

You just need to start with a list.

Start by writing down *everything* you can think of that's still a painful memory. Many people start with their parents and their childhood because those areas often contain a *wealth* of material to forgive, right? Write down every little thing – whether it's something cruel that was said to you, or a traumatic incident that was inflicted upon you. You don't need a special journal and fancy pen (although your procrastination habit might tell you that you do). You can do it on any old scrap of paper.

Here are some ideas for you:

✦ **Old relationships**: write down everything that any of your partners did to make you angry or sad. This is especially important if you were cheated on, a victim of sexual or domestic violence, or were "wronged" in some way. Write down each incident separately.

✦ **Previous jobs**: write down any bosses or colleagues who were mean or intimidating, or who caused you stress in any way. In particular, write down anything they said to you that you still feel strong emotion around.

✦ **Friends or family**: write down anyone who bitched about you, excluded you, or made you feel bad about yourself. Don't forget to include bitchy school friends.

✦ **School**: were there teachers who embarrassed you in front of the whole class, told you were stupid, or unfairly gave you a bad mark?

Whatever comes up, write it all down.

Then, sit somewhere in a quiet space where you won't be disturbed for thirty minutes. In turn, think about each person or situation. If possible, recall what you felt in that moment, whether it was anger, shame, embarrassment, fear, rejection or sadness.

Let the emotion come up around each situation, and then say:

"I forgive you…"

"Thank you…"

"I'm sorry…"

"I love you…"

There are many different ways you can do this, and different orders for the words, but the most important thing is the *intention* behind your words. Please don't get caught up in doing it "perfectly."

How do you know if it's working?

Well, you don't need to force anything, but you may feel emotion or sadness come up. Just let the image of each memory fade away, and then go on to the next one on your list. You don't even really have to 100 percent "mean" each statement you say: your intention is enough to start creating magic in your life.

Some people report having to do the exercise several times for really emotional and painful memories, but each time will clear many years' worth of resentment and anger. This exercise is worth several years in therapy! (Don't get me wrong, therapy is wonderful – and a lot of therapists also encourage the practice of forgiveness.)

Give it a few days, and then check back in with your list to see what memories still remain. You'll be surprised to find that you can't even recall certain "stories." If you do, there probably won't be any trace of embarrassment or anger.

It sounds really unbelievable, but I know this works. I started out with at least three pages' worth of old hurts and injustices; and I honestly couldn't recite the same list to you today. It's almost all gone. The practice has made me more compassionate toward my own parents, too, and the difficulties they must have gone through as young parents who were incompatible, with very little money, and no idea of how to raise children.

What can you expect afterward?

You'll probably find that some things will start to shift in the real world without any other intervention. You'll feel happier and lighter without trying. Don't be surprised if you get a call out of the blue from someone you've forgiven, too (this happens *all the time*). They'll experience the energetic benefits as well – they might feel lighter or more loving toward you without knowing why. You may even feel unexpectedly happy. That feeling was there all along, just waiting until you cleared the energy.

Again, forgiveness *doesn't* mean that you condone the behavior. You don't even have to see the person you're forgiving anymore. It doesn't mean that they've changed, or that it's healthy for you to have them in your life either. But, it does mean that you don't have to live with the pain anymore.

You also won't be seeing that person or situation through a distorted filter – as the person who's responsible for how you feel now – anymore. You'll be free of the chains, and open to new possibilities for your relationship. In fact, you may never even *think* of that person again, which can be a blessing.

Plus, you've given yourself a great gift – freedom.

ARE YOU READY TO EXPERIENCE FREEDOM?

I have a completely transformed relationship now with my own mother. I can listen to her as a happy adult, and not through the filter of an angry, resentful child. I have compassion for the struggles she went through as a single parent, and I can see her as a human being. It makes me more compassionate toward myself as a very imperfect parent, too.

Nothing is too small to forgive. One Lucky Bee forgave a teacher she'd had when she was eight years old, someone who embarrassed her in front of a whole class and set up a lingering fear that she was stupid. Clearing that gave her so much freedom; and the added bonus was that she stopped seeing herself as stupid, too.

When does it end?

Sorry to tell you this, but forgiveness is a life-long process! That said, it becomes a really positive tool that's quick to use, rather than something you have to cry endlessly over or make a ritual out of.

There's no end to forgiveness, but after you get the really traumatic events out of the way, it's fun and so freeing! Forgiveness is like an onion skin. You will *always* find new things to forgive. Always. And that's okay. When you're in the habit, you can do it in minutes, and then quickly move on with your life.

YEAH, YEAH. I KNOW ALL ABOUT FORGIVENESS. YAWN, DENISE.

Feel like you've heard it all before, and have already made peace with the past? Take it one step further, and find new layers to forgive. You'll be surprised by how many little resentments you're holding that add up to wasted energy.

For example: forgive the greedy bankers who ruined the economy during the Global Financial Crisis. Forgive the President or Prime Minister of your country, especially if you didn't vote for them. Forgive the ignorant friends or family who voted for "the other guy." Forgive the corporations who pollute the environment. Forgive your ancestors for passing down cycles of poverty or dysfunction. Forgive, forgive, forgive.

Anywhere you have lingering anger in your life, make a conscious decision to forgive and let it go. It will really transform your life when you release that negative energy... and then watch what happens to your luck!

BUT I DON'T WANT TO FORGIVE, DENISE. CAN'T I SKIP THIS ONE?

No. You can't skip it. But don't worry if you don't have super-traumatic events to forgive – it will still work for you. Dig deep and clear the energy.

Remember: forgiveness is *non-negotiable*. There's no point trying to consciously create outrageous success or happiness for yourself if you skip this step.

2. Get over yourself

OK, hear me out. So you've done the forgiveness work and cleared your slate. That's great. Now it's time to go even deeper into what could be holding you back from the next level of success and happiness. It's not your job or the economy. It's not your age, gender or weight.

Guess what… it's *you*!

Most of us know at a superficial level that the only thing holding us back is ourselves, but we don't realize just how powerful we are. Our ability to protect ourselves from potential pain is incredible. Self-sabotage is a misunderstood creature – it's only trying to keep us from facing rejection! It's the ultimate "helicopter parent," swaddling us in cotton wool so we never injure ourselves in any way.

Unfortunately, we learn by allowing ourselves to experience pain or open ourselves to potential embarrassment. Parents know that eventually they'll have to let their children go out into the big, bad world. Otherwise their kids will turn out to be co-dependent, low-functioning adults who don't know how to do anything for themselves.

Don't allow this to happen to you: set an intention that it's time to get over your fears. Everyone has fears, but the luckiest people are also the ones who just take action *despite their fear*. Lucky people aren't immune to circumstance or failure. They just get more practice, they open themselves to more opportunity, and they don't take every rejection personally.

Your goal isn't to eliminate fear entirely. I'm not sure that's possible or even desirable – after all, sometimes fear can drive us to do things we otherwise wouldn't. However, it's freeing to realize that every human who's ever lived has been just as shit-scared as you are. Everyone. They either just moved forward a tiny bit despite the fear, or they died with regrets.

Barbra Streisand suffered from crippling stage fright for years, which is why she rarely toured at the peak of her career, even though she could have sold out multiple stage dates around the world. However, every few years, she forces herself to get on stage despite the fear. Adele, too. She rarely tours even though she could make a hundred gajillion dollars. Thank Goddess they both overcome their fear every few years. Isn't the world a better place for their talent?

I know many people who are lucky enough to have innate talent, but they're too afraid to do anything about it. I'm talking about people who have incredible manuscripts ready to go, plays written, or unbelievable skills in teaching, cooking or healing… but they're just too scared to let their talent shine. You're a little bit scared too, aren't you? I know I am! *All the time.*

Scared of what?

Maybe you're scared of being so awesome that it will turn you into a diva. Scared of being told you have no talent. Scared of getting constructive feedback from someone you admire, or a bluntly worded rejection. Scared that you'll become famous and get a stalker. Scared that your partner will leave you, or that you'll leave them if you become too successful. Scared that maybe you aren't as smart as you think, and you'll waste your potential. Scared of being told you're too big for your boots.

These are all completely normal fears, by the way, and usually have *nothing* to do with the reality.

Fears like these can be completely irrational and cause you procrastination and self-loathing, but it's time to realize that the fear will never really go away 100 percent – and that that's okay. I'm friends with many successful female millionaires, and they *still* have fears they work on every day. Money doesn't take the fear away.

How I got over my fear of sharks

When I was fourteen, I went swimming with my beloved Nana Judy one day at her local beach. I was an avid swimmer, and – like most kids who grow up near the sea – I loved the ocean life. Swimming was just part of growing up in Australia.

The waves were huge that day; and for a while, Nan and I were trapped out beyond the biggest of them. We were exhausted, but every time we tried to swim for shore, we were pushed back with the waves crashing around us. So we decided to tread water for a while until the ocean calmed down.

Then, in the distance, I saw four dark fins; and in my tired state, I was SURE they were sharks. I started panicking. I thought to myself, *This is how I'm going to die – ripped apart by hungry sharks!*

Nan tried to calm me down, but she was scared, too. There were dark, shark-like rocks underneath us, and I really thought we were gone. I was crying and freaking out. Finally, the waves subsided enough for us to swim to shore; and once we were safely on land, we realized that the fins hadn't belonged to sharks at all.

Instead, they'd belonged to dolphins!

So what *could* have been a beautiful, unique, spiritual experience of swimming with wild dolphins turned into a moment of complete and utter panic. Not only that, but I didn't really go into the water again for the next sixteen years. Honestly. My life-long love of the ocean was gone in minutes. Destroyed completely.

I tried a few times. I could wade in up to my ankles… but then I'd panic, or I'd be scanning the horizon and jumping at any little shadow in the waves. My fear was so irrational that I'd even freak out about going into a swimming pool! (You know, because of the secret trapdoor that lets the sharks in?) Forget about swimming in dark bodies of water like lakes – they obviously had krakens and underwater zombies alongside the sharks!

Even on the Honeymoon Testers' trip, I rarely went into the ocean. We visited some of the most incredible beaches in the world, and I just couldn't relax and enjoy them. I panicked every time I went near the water, even in countries that have never had recorded shark attacks. My fear of being eaten was very real… to me.

In fact, we did a radio interview during the trip; and I was asked if I was going to go snorkeling in Jordan (the Red Sea is famous for amazing sea life). When I said I was afraid of sharks, I could see the interviewer's face, and knew he was thinking *What a waste of an amazing experience – how ungrateful.* And I'm sure many people listening thought the same thing: *She's so lucky! I'd take advantage of every opportunity on that trip.*

This irrational fear really pissed me off. So I tried a few times to enjoy the ocean, but I just freaked out every time. Finally I said, "Universe, please help me with this. I'm ready to overcome my fear now."

The Universe is always listening – so be careful what you ask for. The solution was so much easier than I knew. Sometimes you have just to hitch up your big girl panties and say, "I'm scared but I'm ready." And the Universe *obviously* decided to use this to orchestrate a cure for my fear.

One of the weddings for our Guinness World Record attempt was scheduled to be on a floating pontoon in the middle of the Great Barrier Reef in Queensland. Again, it was an amazing opportunity that would be perfect on a bucket list. I'd seen this listed on the itinerary, but I'd assumed that our pontoon would have a pool in the middle of it, like on a cruise ship.

The idea was that we'd get married on the pontoon, and then we'd jump onto a giant slide together as man and wife, while the photographer captured our landing into the water. Fun, right? Except, when we got there, I realized that the slide went *straight into the ocean.* No netted area. No protected pool. Not even a sandy, clear bottom to be seen: because it was a cloudy day, the ocean was a dark green color.

Oh. My. God. It was my worst nightmare! In Australia, no less – the land of the Great White Shark. We were in the sharkiest sea in the sharkiest shark-ridden country on the planet.

I could have said, "No, I'm afraid of the water. I'm not going to do it." But instead, I knew it was time to kick this fear to the curb. It had to be done, and there was no *way* I'd make a scene. My fear of embarrassing myself was greater than my fear of sharks that day; and I just hoped that if a shark came along, it'd eat Mark (or a slow tourist/grandma) first. That's what I told myself anyway.

So as we stood there, getting married in front of the Captain, I really regretted watching every shark movie ever made, as well as reading *Jaws* when I was younger.

I stuck a smile on my face for the whole wedding, gripping Mark's hands very tightly. I felt sick to my stomach. Then we got onto the slide and posed for a photo, and all the while I was freaking out. The photographer gave us a count-down, and off we went – down the slide, and into the dark green water of the most shark-infested ocean on the planet. (Okay, I totally made that up; but in my mind, there were hungry Great Whites down there about to eat me up.)

I immediately came up for air, dragging my wedding veil behind me, and swam quickly back to the pontoon. As soon as we got out of the water, I high-fived Mark: I'd done it! I was so happy to cross that off the itinerary.

My celebration lasted until the photographer approached us with a frown on his face. "Denise," he said, "Your hand was covering Mark's face. You'll have to do it again."

Are you kidding me? You're going to dangle me in front of sharks again!?

Again, though, I decided to just bite the bullet. The photographer was from Getty. There was a small crowd watching us, and I've *never* been one to cry in public. *Suck it up, Denise! The show must go on.*

The second time down the slide was easier; but don't forget that I was wearing a short, white wedding dress and a veil, plus a full face of makeup. My hair was already ruined from the first take and my dress was see-through, but my adrenaline was *through the roof*.

And guess what? The second take wasn't good enough either. *Argh! Universe, are you trying to kill me?*

No, I told myself. This was a valuable lesson. You need to get over yourself. Your fear isn't real.

We did the "slide into the deep ocean" thing *five times* before we got it right: there was something wrong with each shot. And *then* the photographer requested some underwater photos meters away from the safety of the pontoon – literally in the middle of the ocean. No problem, right? Whatever you need! The obedient "good girl" part of me that didn't want to say no overcame my fear, and I've actually never been more grateful for her.

Even though I was terrified at the start, after a while, repeating the scary action made it… less scary.

And by the end of that day, I was cured. *Cured* of sixteen years of terror. In fact, later that day, I actually snorkeled with Mark and saw little clown fish that looked exactly like they do in *Finding Nemo*. We watched a green turtle fly off into the distance. It was truly life-changing, and I know the Universe orchestrated that situation for me, because I told it that I was ready. (Remember, the mantra "It's my time and I'm ready for the next step.") Hilariously, one of our next weddings was actually standing in a stingray enclosure while an actual shark circled us in the water. Just to make sure I got the message. Thanks Universe!

Was it a permanent cure for my fear? Yes.

Okay, I *still* can't face the underwater zombies in cloudy river water, but the ocean? No problem.

Now I live in a sunny seaside town; and I'm happy to say that every summer, Mark and I swim almost every day in the ocean with our kids. It's the most liberating experience, riding waves and getting lost in my own thoughts while connecting to the power of water. I'm never going to swim really far out, and I won't be swimming with sharks anytime soon; but I can now enjoy the ocean like the water baby I was born to be.

Overcoming that fear has been so symbolic for me, and it's unraveled many other fears, too. If I can swim in the ocean, I can do anything! I've absorbed that lesson of forcing myself to overcome my fears, and it's now my main strategy for making big leaps.

Use your tools!

So what can you learn from this? There are literally *no* fears that you cannot overcome. There are also many tools and pathways to get there: you just need to find what works for you.

My favorite tool now seems to be the "no way out" scenario, because it works with my personality. I don't like letting people down, and I can always perform in public if I need to. I think this comes from my dance career, where – no matter what happens – the show *must* go on, even if you just twisted your ankle or your leotard is wedged up your butt.

When I find myself scared of public speaking, I'll book a workshop date or a teleseminar, and then (and this is the crucial part) actually *advertise* it on my website. This public commitment is a very powerful tool. It's also a great strategy, because I know I'll show up and deliver no matter what. My fear of making an idiot of myself is outweighed by the fear of letting someone else down. I won't turn up unprepared, so I'll be forced to just do it.

This is a much more effective strategy than just hoping that you'll "feel like it." Trust me: if I only did my business when I "felt like it," I wouldn't have a business, let alone a successful one.

But guess what else? You don't have to eliminate your fear altogether for it to count as a success. I still get nervous before I speak on stage. I still worry that the tech will fail just before a teleseminar. And that's okay. *The absence of fear isn't the goal.* Living your best life (despite the fear) is what you're aiming for.

I'm still scared of sharks, but I'm more willing to enjoy the beauty of the ocean because I know the rewards, and I understand what I'll miss out on. The chances of me being eaten by sharks is greater in the water than if I stay on the sand, but it's still very slight overall. (And I *always* make sure there's someone further out from the shore than me, just in case).

Honestly, most of our biggest fears are total BS. And overcoming the crippling effects of your fear won't stop "bad" things from occasionally happening to you. Just because I overcame my fear of sharks enough to swim in the ocean, it doesn't mean that I'm magically immune to being stung by a jellyfish or getting sunburnt. Risk is human.

Ditto with *any* irrational fear. The chances of a potential publishing house telling you that you're horrible and have no talent are pretty small, but that doesn't mean you won't face rejection. (Hopefully it'll be more polite, though.)

Does that mean you should never submit your book proposal? After all, a certain amount of rejection is normal and virtually inevitable. The important thing is what you do *after* you get your first rejection. Do you give up, or just send the next one?

What looks like luck from the outside is often merely the willingness to do what other people don't have the guts to do. Most wannabe actors don't audition nearly enough. Most aspiring writers never send their work out to be published, and most women don't get pay increases because they simply don't ask for them.

This isn't being simplistic. There's definitely a huge amount of discrimination in the opportunities that women and minorities have access to. But I want you to be honest – have you *really* tried hard enough? Are you playing the numbers game, or did you give up after the very first "no?"

> *"Any fool can have bad luck; the art*
> *consists in knowing how to exploit it."*
> FRANK WEDEKIND

So, let's really get real about *your* fears. You might love public speaking, and you've never worried about sharks, but maybe your fears are completely different from mine.

Take the time to get really specific about exactly what you're scared of.

Why is it so important to acknowledge your fears?

Isn't it negative to dwell on what you don't want? After all, it seems that the self-help industry wants us to be endlessly upbeat *all the time.*

Absolutely, we should focus *mostly* on the positive vibes that we want to create in the world. I'm definitely not encouraging you to wallow in misery. However, until you face your fears, you won't see the patterns that you may have been repeating over and over in your life. These patterns have trapped you, and you need to break through them to get to the other side.

In other words – you need to get over yourself.

✧ *Action step* ✧
Get over your fears.

Grab your journal. Start writing about the fears that come up when you think about all your goals coming true. If you get stuck, use the following as prompts:

- If I achieve this goal, I'm afraid that…

- To achieve this goal, I'll have to do things I'm scared of, like…

- What's the very worst thing that could happen if I…?

- These people will hate me if I'm successful…

Get specific. Until you acknowledge something, you won't be able to clear it. Sometimes, you might find really irrational fears, like:

- If I'm successful, I'll lose all my friends.

- If my business makes money, my husband will feel emasculated and leave me.

- If I'm successful at work, that makes me a bad mother to my kids.

- I can either have love or money, but I can't have both.

Sometimes, even just writing a fear down will make you say to yourself, *Really?! Do I really believe that shit?* Seriously. It will sound as silly as thinking, *If I go into a swimming pool, a secret tunnel will open up and a shark will eat me.*

How do you deal with those fears? Well – I have lots of tips for you in this book; but often, the most powerful tool is awareness:

❖ Awareness that you're making up negative consequences

❖ Awareness that you're allowing irrational fears to ruin your dreams

❖ Awareness that you have the power to overcome your fears.

And that awareness really is the best start.

3. Be grateful

Gratitude is a powerful force for manifestation; and it can transform your perspective of the world in an instant. It's another common-to-the-point-of-cliché personal development tool, and for good reason. Gratitude is not complacency about what you have, but neither is it about creating pure perfection.

At every stage of your success journey, you've got to embrace what you have now. Otherwise, it will never be enough, and you'll be an ungrateful, spoilt brat like Veruca Salt in the story *Charlie and the Chocolate Factory* – always wanting the next shiny object, *now, Daddy!*

Leaders like Oprah and Dr. John Demartini credit a regular practice of gratitude for the abundance they've been able to create. Oprah inspired the world to keep daily gratitude journals, and Demartini wrote more than one book on the regular practice of giving thanks.

The Universe responds to our feelings, and mirrors our reality in line with those powerful emotions. So when we focus on lack, we attract more lack. Have you noticed that when you feel crappy about money, you often manifest more bills? And when you're on a roll in business, you attract even *more* clients?

It often feels like a gamble, though, because we're waiting for the outside reality to change before we decide how we feel about it. We think, *Okay, Universe, send me something good, and* **then** *I'll feel grateful about my life!* Or we think, *I'll wait for this horrible situation to pass, and* **then** *I'll get back on track with my gratitude practice.*

It's a chicken and egg scenario.

So how do you change your mindset when the reality isn't there yet? You have to practice radical, unrelenting, uncompromising gratitude, *no matter what* – and if you can't find something to be grateful for, you're not trying hard enough.

That sounds harsh, but what's the alternative? Do you want your situation to change or not? You can wait for the Universe to do it for you; or you can take the quickest, easiest route, and take responsibility for your feelings.

When you focus on the amazing abundance and opportunity around you, you activate the unseen forces in the Universe that are intent on matching your vibration with even more. Being grateful brings you more abundance, because you recognize and appreciate the abundance that you already have in your life.

The opposite of gratitude is being thankless, rude, and unmindful. This shows that you're unaware of what's truly possible. You're like an ignorant tourist, breaking everything, and consuming resources with abandon –

not caring, and not even enjoying the experience. You're never, ever happy with what you have – and trust me, no amount of money can change that feeling.

I know it's difficult to be grateful when your "reality" seems so real. The goldfish can't see the water – he's in it. When you're *in* your experience of being in debt, or in a horrible job, or lonely on a Saturday night, all you can feel is the pain of your experience. That makes it hard to cultivate gratitude!

Often, you can't even see what there might be to be grateful for.

> YOU DON'T UNDERSTAND DENISE – MY EXPERIENCE IS REAL. MY BANK ACCOUNT *IS* EMPTY, I DON'T HAVE ANY MONEY, AND I REALLY *AM* HAVING THIS EXPERIENCE!

Yes, that might be true. But how much *longer* do you want it to be real? What's your solution to get out of it? Gratitude is free, and it works. Your situation might not change overnight, but you can feel better about it in an instant.

There is always, *always* something to be grateful for.

I'm here to tell you that the only way out of a crappy situation is to change your perception and find the silver lining. Otherwise, you'll be stuck there forever. And when you *feel* better about your situation, you might free up some energy to actually do something about it.

Again, I totally understand that it can be hard. We invest a lot into defending our "right way" of thinking. Sometimes your situation feels like *the worst* – but that doesn't mean that it's true. And if *I* managed to do it, and thousands of Lucky Bees around the world have managed it, too, I promise you that so can you.

That's why I love the Internet. You can literally find millions of stories of people overcoming the worst situations. If they can do it, why not you?

Gratitude can transform the past. When I focused on the positives of my childhood – for example, the independence I gained from my mother's relaxed attitude to parenting – it completely transformed my experience of it. When I forgave my parents, and then found things about my childhood that have benefited me today, I no longer thought I'd had a "bad childhood," but that I'd had an awesome one, for *me*. I chose to look at my situation from a different perspective: one of gratitude for the good parts, rather than resentment for the bad. How did I do it? I started with forgiveness, took responsibility to get over myself, and then focused on the positives of the experience. It changed my life.

✧ Action step ✧

Start being grateful now.

Take out your journal again, and ask yourself:

✤ What are you grateful for in your life right now?

- ✦ What are you grateful about with your health?

- ✦ What gratitude can you express about your relationships?

- ✦ What aspects of the past can you now be grateful about?

One of the best ways to increase your luck and capacity for good fortune is to treat yourself like you're already blessed in every way. The thing is that you are!

Don't believe me? Try it.

4. Treat yourself like a VIP

Are you cheap with yourself, or do you treat yourself like a Very Important Person? I used to be so embarrassingly stingy with myself that I never let myself even *look* in the window of a shop. I certainly didn't let myself dream that I was worth more.

A lot of people are broke while they're studying: I'm not unique in that experience. It's kind of a rite of passage, but I took it to an extreme level. Not only that, but I made it mean that I was an unworthy person, who was worth less than other people.

For six months, I lived in an outdoor laundry that had been converted into a room (of sorts), with no furniture but a single bed and some stacked milk crates for my clothes. It didn't even have proper windows: instead, there was just a metal grate with clear plastic sheeting over it.

This "room" cost me $50 a week, which was cheap, even in 1998; but I felt like such a loser coming home to it each day. I was failing in my studies. I was depressed. I had no money, and I lived in a *shed!* I once even brought a guy back to that shed. *Could it get any worse?*

The trouble was that I had no minimum standards for myself. I accepted whatever circumstances I could "afford" without demanding anything different.

In my twenties, I often dressed in cheap, ill-fitting clothes because I thought caring about my appearance was superficial. In reality, my stinginess with myself just made me feel bad. Plus, it takes up valuable energy to disguise a missing button or hide a stain. Have you ever experienced those kinds of mental gymnastics? It's exhausting!

I was no longer a "poor kid," but I was still energetically locked in that pattern.

Oprah said something once that stuck with me. Apparently, billionaires still sniff their workout shirts to see if they can wear them again (just like us!). She realized she was doing it one day, and said to herself, *I deserve to wear a fresh, clean shirt. I'm worth it.*

Now, Oprah can afford to change her clothes every hour if she wants to, but the story isn't about the shirt. It's about treating yourself like you matter.

I once told this story about Oprah at a workshop and then during the break, I went to refresh my cup of tea; and as I was adding more hot water, I suddenly realized, *"I'm totally worth a fresh tea bag!"* Peppermint tea isn't quite as nice the second time around, right? It sounds silly, but I actually teared up a little, because I finally got the message for myself. I utterly believe that great success comes down to self-worth. You show other people how to treat you by the way you treat yourself; but you also send a very strong message to the Universe that you deserve and are ready for more.

You're worth it. You deserve whatever you want to create in the world. You matter.

I totally believe in not being wasteful, but many women take the whole self-sacrificing thing way too far. I should know – I once didn't wash my hair for over six months!

That's right. I experimented with "no-poo," which means you stop using conventional shampoos, and let your hair naturally cleanse itself instead. You can use natural ingredients like baking soda, flax seeds, and lemon, but it takes a while for your hair to adjust. It was kind of… gross.

It started out being about the environment; but really, it was the ultimate in self-denial. After my hair adjusted itself and looked semi-decent, I decided to stop using anything and just wash my hair with water, which started the process all over again. How much pleasure could I strip away? How much further could I go?

It wasn't nice, and it certainly wasn't pretty. But I was determined to stick it out for more than six months. Why? I don't know. I was stubborn, I guess; and maybe deep down, I didn't believe I deserved to have an easy life.

So you might not have smelly hair, but here are some clues that you're treating yourself like a poor relation:

❀ You only shop in thrift stores when other people in your family get newer and nicer clothes, because you feel bad about spending the money.

✦ You try to do something yourself (like dye your hair or tint your own eyelashes) with disastrous results.

✦ You save your fancy beauty products "for best," or never use your favorite things like pretty tea cups or nice stationery.

✦ You keep clothes, shoes or bags that are old, need repairs, or are out of date because they're "better than nothing."

None of these things are "bad" in themselves (for example, I love buying vintage furniture). It's how each thing *makes you feel* that's the problem.

Maybe you're already wildly successful in one area of your life, so you'd feel guilty if you were great at everything. What would your friends think if you not only had money, but were really super-healthy as well? Or if you had a great marriage *and* a successful business? What a lucky bitch!

Well, I'm here to tell you that you *can* have it all. No guilt and no sacrifice required. You just have to decide that you're worth an amazing life.

But… it starts with you. The Universe isn't going to treat you like a VIP until you treat yourself that way. Extreme self-care and outrageous self-love are *crucial* secrets of successful women; and those women don't wait for either one to be offered to them on a silver platter. Instead, they create what they need for themselves.

This is not only about spending money. It's also about having an attitude of abundance, feeling okay about increasing your expectation of minimum standards, and constantly raising the bar for yourself.

One of my biggest annoyances is the overuse of the word "luxury" when it comes to products sold to women. Next time you're watching TV, just notice how many ordinary, everyday, cheap, and downright boring products are sold using language such as "treat yourself." It's not gorgeous shoes or spa days either. Instead, it's household items like dishwashing liquid, air freshener spray, and body wash; as if we women should be *grateful* to spend five minutes soaping up our bodies, and as if it's the highlight of our day. The message is, "*Be busy, expect less, and feel guilty about spending five bucks on yourself.*"

I understand that when you're a mother to young children, having a shower definitely IS a luxury some days (and I know I *love* long showers by myself). But women, please – don't we deserve more than just enjoying a cheap consumer product? Have you ever *actually* had an orgasm over shower gel? (And if so, please tell me which brand, so I can try it out for myself!) Do you really admire your nails and soft hands after washing the dishes? Most people would prefer to get a real manicure!

Chocolate isn't an "indulgent treat," and unless you're buying gold-flecked chocolate, it's not even that expensive. If you want some, just have some – and enjoy it. Buy yourself a magazine because it's cheap and provides a bit of entertainment, not because it somehow gives you "me time" and you think you *should*. Just do it.

Do men have "me time" that they need to explain, justify or feel guilty over?!

Real luxury is being attuned to your self-worth, allowing yourself to have the job you want, spending time with the people you like, and being challenged and entertained in the way you enjoy. Luxury is being free to do what you want, when you want to do it. And luxury *isn't* found in the cleaning aisle of the supermarket, no matter what advertisers want us to believe.

The truth is that having a really clean, shiny toilet is not that deeply satisfying to my soul. Plugging in an artificial air freshener does not make me want to dance around my house in ecstasy. Honestly, with all these mixed messages, it's no wonder that women feel guilty or "selfish" for wanting more in life.

Winning the Honeymoon Testers' competition definitely increased my capacity for luxury, and showed me how rich people lived. Yes, it's comfortable to have someone to run you a bath, pack your luggage for you, and order you a limousine. It's amazing. But some things get boring – like having rose petals arranged on your bed every day, or getting yet another bottle of free champagne. That might sound diva-ish, but it's true. It's not real, deep luxury that you feel in your soul – it's fake and unsatisfying. In fact, I realized that I didn't even *like* champagne that much. And it's annoying brushing rose petals off your bed every day! #luckybitchproblems

Over the last few years, after exploring what real luxury means to me, I've noticed that upgrading my everyday experiences feels better than "fake" luxury or things that TV has told me I should care about.

Having time off to read a book in the sunshine, drinking tea out of a special mug, and swimming in the ocean are all things I once denied myself, citing lack of time or guilt. I denied myself VIP treatment, because I felt I had to somehow "deserve" it, or that it was virtuous to be rushed and stressed every day. I felt that I didn't even deserve simple things like changing my sheets regularly or wearing my favorite perfume. I'm more interested these days in creating real richness, instead of fake luxury. And that includes creating more space, to just... be.

Many women feel like they have to be busy all the time, or they'll feel lazy. That's BS. Being busy doesn't mean you're effective or efficient. In fact, it can mean the exact opposite. Would a VIP allow herself to be rushed or stressed? Maybe once in a while, when the deadlines got close; but definitely not every day.

Start blocking out small pockets of VIP "freedom" time to enjoy in your day. I bet you'll feel amazing when you do, and you already know that you attract more of what you feel, so start today!

David Neagle, a self-help author and money coach, says he made a decision that he'd only fly First Class, no matter what – and the money always appears. I've also heard Ali Brown, coach for women entrepreneurs, say the same thing. I was too chicken to go straight to First Class, so I started with small upgrades like extra leg room and priority boarding. Then I set an intention to only fly Premium Economy or above. You might not be able to stomach going from the cheapest ticket to First Class every time, but you can work your way incrementally toward it. I had to acclimatize to First Class, not only the cost but the experience of it. That flying First Class was something "someone like me" could do as no big deal.

Before I could afford it, I decided to always buy the VIP upgrade option at personal development and networking conferences. It's worth the money to have all the little extras, like priority seating and free lunch. The option usually includes a private networking event with the speaker, or a photo opportunity with them, too. It's just a decision I made, so I can stop worrying about whether I'll upgrade or not. I'm a VIP, so of course I'll choose that option.

Decide to constantly upgrade your life. Incrementally, and with the things that feel the most symbolic to you.

I used to dye my hair myself, so I made a decision to always go to a proper salon, which might be a no-brainer to you, but I felt like it was out of reach for a long time for me. It makes me feel amazing to have great hair, and it's a small price to pay to feel like a VIP. Similarly, when I have a conference or speaking engagement, I'll always get my hair professionally blow-dried.

Good hair was always *the* thing I couldn't spend money on because I felt guilty and superficial, but learning to embrace the upgrade has completely changed my business for the better. When I have good hair, I seem to take more action, like making videos or live-streaming to my audience. So this upgrade actually makes me money. Your thing might be a pedicure or laser hair removal – anything that makes you feel more confident.

What's the next upgrade you can make?

There's a difference between being frugal and being downright cheap with yourself. You probably have a drawer full of expensive beauty products that you never use, beautiful underwear that never sees the light of day, and favorite shoes that are saved for "best."

What if every day was your best?

✦ *Action* ✦

Increase your pleasure threshold!

What's the next level of self-care, luxury or indulgence for you? Make a decision. Decide in advance how much of your income you'll spend solely on yourself. I recommend at least 10 percent to start with, especially if you're not used to it. Remember, you have to acclimatize to it. Dedicate that money to pleasure and celebration so you can increase your pleasure threshold. Ten percent isn't too much to ask, is it? The rules: the money can't be spent on mundane things like underwear (unless it's gorgeous lingerie); practical personal care products like tampons that you'd buy anyway; or anything for your children, partner or friends.

Get real about what luxury means to you.

Decide to treat yourself like a superstar, and watch your luck and success soar. I personally guarantee it, and I look forward to seeing you in the VIP lounge.

We need a secret Lucky Bee handshake!

Consciously celebrate your success

Do you reward yourself when you complete a project, get a new article published, or sell a piece of work? Or do you move on to the next thing, telling yourself it was no big deal? Um – I know *I'm* guilty as charged. Well, I'm much more conscious about acknowledging success these days (and writing about it in this book is living proof!), but I used to be the WORST. I told myself that a success didn't count if it wasn't perfect, or that I'd only feel good about my success when I really *deserved* it.

Now, though, I celebrate!

Celebrate every milestone, because it anchors the experience into your subconscious – and then you'll attract even more when you feel worthy and successful. Find any excuse to congratulate yourself for a job well done. Success breeds success, and the more "proof" you have that you're doing well, the easier it will be to attract further good fortune.

This is hugely important if you're at the start of your business. You almost have to go *overboard* and exaggerate the celebrations.

When I started my business (with zero clients, like everyone else), I did a lot of work for free – including discovery sessions, practice sessions with clients in exchange for testimonials, and lots of free events.

Then, when I ran my first paid one-day workshop, I made sure I celebrated. It was a huge deal to make money out of something I loved... even though, to be honest, I didn't make that much profit out of it. In fact, if I'd calculated my actual hourly rate for the event – let alone the effort I'd put into it – it would have come out as a few cents per hour.

BUT, I was still thrilled; and I knew that I had to celebrate like crazy and anchor in the feeling of accomplishment and pride.

I was incredibly tired after the event, but I went to the poshest restaurant in town: a place that would normally intimidate me. However, I was wearing new clothes and had fabulous hair because I'd treated myself to a professional blow dry for the event; so I walked in like I belonged there, and ordered a single glass of expensive champagne. I literally had to check my bank account balance on my phone to see if I could afford some snacks to go with the champagne, so I ordered poutine even though I wasn't quite sure what it was, it just sounded fancy. Then I sat there alone, just letting myself soak in the experience and told myself, *This is just the beginning. Well done, babe!*

The event was a workshop of twenty-five people – not a huge deal in the grand scheme of my business, but it was something I'd created by myself. It wasn't perfect, but I'd put it together with passion and commitment. I knew that I'd done my best, so I knew I deserved to enjoy it, and I promptly reminded the Universe that it was a big deal!

Honestly, I've had lots of successes in my business since that day, but that felt pretty *damn* amazing. It felt much more symbolic than hitting the six-figure mark, and even better than hitting a million dollars.

Being an entrepreneur is not for the faint of heart – so you have to give yourself every chance to succeed and keep working, even when the results are slow. If I hadn't celebrated all of those early successes, I doubt I would have had the guts to keep going. Too many people give up early because they feel discouraged, often by the lack of support from other people in their lives.

You have to be your best cheerleader. Celebrating an experience in a memorable way gives you permission to be richly rewarded for your efforts. It shows the Universe how to treat you, and it puts you in a success mindset. Don't let your moment of celebration pass you by unacknowledged: buy yourself a nice piece of jewelry or special shoes, or do whatever makes YOU feel like you're celebrating; and really anchor that experience within yourself.

5. Get your boobs on board

When I was at university, I decided to do something that really challenged my perception of my body. I posed nude for an art class. It was one of the most liberating experiences of my life, because it made me accept my body. Not only that, but it also let me see my body through other people's eyes.

As women, we experience so much hatred of ourselves and our bodies; and it can really hold us back in many areas of our lives. In every fiber of our being, we are saying, "You're not worth more!" or, "I'll only deserve it when I'm... (thin/tidier/more focused/married)."

The next step after forgiving everyone else is to forgive yourself and love your body, no matter what. A revolutionary exercise is to repeat the forgiveness mantra for *yourself*. Forgive your mistakes and your humanity, and be compassionate.

How can you live a truly exceptional life when you unconsciously infuse every part of your being with judgments such as, "*You are wrong, you are ugly, you are fat, you are too hairy, you are not right in some fundamental way, you are not perfect!"* These judgments permeate your entire body *and* your entire soul.

How can you live a beautiful life, creating exactly what you want, when you're carrying that kind of negativity?

Let me tell you a story about my past.

When I was twelve, I had this fabulous tie-dyed rainbow dress. I wore it to my Year Six formal, but I wanted to wear it all the time (in the way that twelve-year-olds do), even though it was getting way too short and tight.

One time, I wore it to the grocery store. I was just running in to get something for my mother, and I looked really scruffy. I wasn't wearing any shoes, because I'd came straight from playing in my back yard, and my curly hair was all over the place. I was just on the cusp of being a teenager but I was still a fairly unselfconscious kid.

As I walked through the aisles, I noticed this family staring at me in disgust. They obviously thought I was some homeless kid; and from outside appearances, I probably looked really rough. I suddenly became aware of how I looked, and felt completely ashamed. Instead of being a carefree twelve-year-old wearing her favorite dress, it dawned on me how inappropriately I was dressed.

I ran into the family again a couple of aisles down, and their little daughter said "Look, Daddy, there's that girl again!"

I wanted the ground to swallow me up. *"That girl."* Like I was something disgusting and "other" from this nice, normal family. I felt so terrible inside, and SO deeply ashamed. I already had an inferiority complex about being raised by a single parent and not having a lot of money, but now I also had this feeling of, "*You are bad, you are dirty, and you're a bad girl.*"

I was only an innocent child wearing an admittedly inappropriate dress; but for *years* I carried those words with me. No matter what successes I had in my life, inside I was still "*that girl.*" This was only a snapshot in time, but it affected me as an adult.

I made it mean that there was something wrong with me.

You may not be aware of the judgments you have of yourself; so you need to figure them out, and get off the judgment train.

Shame lives in every cell of your body. All of those old memories live inside you, and often pop up when you're doing important work – like just before you launch a new service or upgrade your life.

You know those little whispers you sometimes get that say, *You are a bad person. You don't deserve a good life!?* Yup – we all have them.

So what do your boobs have to do with this?

A great way to release these feelings of shame is to do body forgiveness. I go into this in much more depth later in this book. For the meantime, however, realize that forgiveness can permeate throughout your whole body. It can get every cell of your body on board – including your boobs. Boobs were the most symbolic part for me, because for years, I was ashamed about having nipple hair (I wish the Internet was around so I could have felt normal that other people have it, too). Your symbolic body part might be your stomach, the stretch marks on your thighs, your neck, etc.

You can do your body forgiveness work in *exactly* the same way that you forgive other people. As you're drifting off to sleep at night, go through each area of your body in turn and say, "Toes, I forgive you. Thank you. I'm sorry. I love you." Then work your way through every body part to the top of your head.

Feel that love and acceptance in every single cell of your body. Realize that you're not perfect and that's okay, but you *are* loved – every last imperfect, gorgeous bit of you.

Do the exercise again, and give an outrageous compliment to each part of your body. Praise your beautiful hair, your perfectly shaped lips, and your lovely shoulders. Inform every cell that you're a gorgeous, exceptional woman; and you expect them all to behave accordingly!

I do this exercise regularly, and have for years. Sometimes the negativity of the world, or the expectations I put on myself set up this anxiety and fear that I'm actually a terrible, useless person. So, I do this activity to remind myself that I'm normal and human. It's okay for me to experience love and extraordinary luck.

How much could you create once your boobs/tummy/thighs are on board with your dreams? When your toes feel like part of the team that's creating your awesome life? When your stretch marks feel fully accepted?

This one exercise will change your life.

It may sound weird, but when every single cell of your body aligns in the direction of your dreams, the whole

Universe screams, "Yes! Yes! *You love us; we love you; let's do it!*" But when you live in the constant reality of "*I'm not perfect,*" every part of your body drags you down and scatters your energy.

Get your boobs on board the luck train. Whoo, whoo!

6. Some people will think you suck: get over it

Worried that people might not like what you do? That you'll get criticized? I'm really sorry, but there's nothing you can do to avoid this. In a popularity poll, not even Mother Teresa would get a 100 percent approval rating. Yet we keep trying, don't we?

The truth is that women who let themselves shine and achieve a certain level of success *will* attract a small amount of negativity. There will *always* be some smartass who thinks you're a lucky bitch with no talent. It happens to me all the time, and it honestly doesn't bother me anymore. It's going to happen if you're unsuccessful, and it's going to happen if you're extremely successful. So which situation would you rather be in?

I'm an extremely opinionated person, but that doesn't mean I'm always right (I'm *frequently* right, however). Ditto with the people in your life. Just because they have an opinion on how you should live your life, or run your business – well, you know what we said in the last chapter about opinions!

Nobody really has the right to tell you their opinion on what you're doing unless they've done the exact same thing you want to do. Even if they have, if they did it twenty, ten, or even five years ago, times have changed since then. Helpful advice is always welcome of course. What I'm talking about here, though, is uninformed people making blanket declarations or asking concern-trolling questions designed to make you feel unsure and anxious about your decisions. Things like…

❖ "You can't make it in showbiz because you're too short."

❖ "Don't you need a degree for that?"

❖ "You're not qualified enough."

❖ "There's no money in that."

❖ "I tried that once – it didn't work for me."

People who say these things always sound like they know what they're talking about because they're so damn *sure* of themselves. I advise you to take their comments with a pinch of salt. I'm sure you've said similar things before without really meaning them, so don't take the opinions of others as gospel, especially if the people sharing them aren't doing the exact thing you want to do.

On the other side of the coin, many of us find it painfully hard to hear feedback, even when we ask for it. I used to *hate* sending out a survey at the end of a course or coaching, because I was often afraid of what people would say. I know it's stupid, because that feedback would make the course better next time, but I don't want to hear that people *don't like me*.

Lots of women are like this, because we take other people's opinions so personally.

And just because someone puts something on the Internet doesn't mean it's true!

It can be shocking how unsupportive and downright bitchy other people can be when your life starts to take off. You'll start to get all sorts of well-meaning "advice," which is often criticism or jealousy in disguise.

Truth time: entrepreneurship isn't always easy.

Nothing brings up our worst fears and insecurities like going into business for ourselves; and it's easy to give away your power and energy so that other people will like you and not feel threatened by your success.

It goes back to our earliest, most primitive fears of being ostracized or rejected from the tribe – being sent away alone to die by ourselves or get eaten by... I don't know... dinosaurs or something. Anyone who's been "mean-girled" in high school dreads that feeling; and it can affect your ability to create success in your life now as a grown woman, too.

Nobody wants to be rejected from their tribe.

Leading an exceptional or unconventional life can feel really threatening to other people. That's why I'm telling you that it's inevitable that you'll be criticized at some point, possibly even by people who are supposed to be loved ones. But that's *their* stuff. It's not yours. What they think of you is none of your business. What they think of your business – well, it's literally not *their* business at all, is it?

What about Internet trolls and haters? Yeah, they're not fun, but they also happen way less than you fear they will.

It's totally irrational, but most of us worry far more about what random strangers say than what our loved ones do. After all, your best friend or parents are unlikely to say outright, "You suck and you have no talent." People on the Internet – on the other hand – will, and do!

This is a comment I received on my blog way back when…

Hi Denise,

I enjoy reading about your success – although I would like to offer a piece of wisdom – that when things are going your way, you give back out. It's important to remember the fine line of narcissism when manifesting – everything is coming to me etc… it's all about me. Doing things for free can keep you grounded and avoid looking like you expect everyone to conform to your wishes (especially when you are successfully manifesting) and it reminds oneself that all these things come from Grace and not "Me" or "My Precious" as Gollum puts it.

People like that *love* to give their criticism in the form of "wisdom" or "advice." That's because it makes them sound like they're really concerned about you, rather than the truth that they're triggered by your success, and unwilling to take responsibility for their own thoughts.

I have to admit that this "offering" really pissed me off. Firstly, because nobody wants to think that they come off as bragging or being narcissistic (or to think they sound like Gollum, for God's sake!); and secondly – how fucking rude to send someone an email like this!

I actually decided not to read any of my bad press or hate mail soon after this: in fact, I don't really do email *at all* these days. My assistant filters everything now. I might get reams of hate mail and not even know about it!

The thing to ask yourself is how it serves your life to read someone's random and often totally irrational opinion. That opinion is very rarely constructive.

But Denise! How am I supposed to stay humble and in touch with my tribe??? Trust me, there are ways to do that other than to read your hate mail. You don't need to take on everyone's opinions to get a flavor of what needs to be improved in your business.

You also don't have to run your business in a way that accommodates everyone's individual preferences. Your personal attention is valuable, so save it for your customers. Someone else can take care of the initial response to random strangers and point them in the right direction.

Remember: your only job is to keep your vibes positive. You have to protect your energy like it's a precious and rare resource, because it is!

> *"I believe in luck: how else can you explain the success of those you dislike?"*
> Jean Cocteau

The first piece of negative feedback you receive can be devastating, but it's the *fear* of the potential criticism that can cut the most. As Mark Twain said, *"I've known many troubles in my life – most of which never happened."*

When the criticism happens, it probably won't be as bad as you think. In fact, I encourage you to consider it a badge of honor – an indicator that you're becoming really successful. Lucky Bees in my Bootcamp report in from all around the world to celebrate their first haters as proof that they're making progress to success!

To illustrate this story, I went searching for Amazon reviews on commercially successful books. Take Lauren Weisberger's first novel, *The Devil Wears Prada*. I loved this book and found it a great, fun, summer read. It's not a literary masterpiece; but if you'd written it, wouldn't you be proud of its obvious commercial success?

Let's face it: *The Devil Wears Prada* has sold millions of copies, spent more than a year on the New York Times bestseller list, and has been made into a fabulously fun movie that grossed over $300 million worldwide and starred Anne Hathaway and Meryl Streep (who won a Golden Globe for the role, *thank you very much*). I'd bet Lauren's parents and friends are really proud.

However, I also hope she has a thick skin. The official Amazon reviewer calls her *"an inept, ungrammatical writer;"* and out of over a thousand reviews, Lauren has more one-star reviews than five-star ones. Do you think she reads the negative ones and regrets ever putting herself out there for public scrutiny?

I doubt it, because she's written at least six other books. She probably had a good cry after reading the reviews – just like anyone would – but she kept writing more books. She didn't let the criticism stop her from making her impact on the world.

Don't you think she was thrilled about her novel being made into a movie? Can you imagine how exciting that would be?! But *we* want that kind of success without any downside, right?

Well, maybe Lauren felt a little less excited when, on the DVD commentary, the screenwriter basically said that the source material wasn't great, and that she'd had to make a lot of changes to make it barely watchable. I'm paraphrasing dramatically there, but *ouch!*

Can you accept that a certain level of success will inevitably attract *some* bad reviews, even if the majority of people loved it?

Which option below would you prefer?

❖ **Option 1:** Ten people buy your "great work," and they all love it. Every single person (which includes a big percentage of your friends and family) has only great things to say about it. Yay for you! You have a 100 percent approval rating! Yep… and you're probably also *broke*, because you stayed in your safe little bubble. But hey, everyone loves you!

❖ **Option 2:** A thousand people (or more) buy your book, come and see your play, buy your artwork, or come to your workshop. The majority of these people are strangers to you. Thirty people say it's the best thing they've ever seen in their whole life, and 940 people seemed to have enjoyed it… but those remaining thirty people say it's the worst thing they've ever seen. They write about it viciously on their blogs, giving you *zero* stars, and they publicly vow it was a waste of money. A couple even ask for a refund, and swear that you're a terrible con artist with no talent. And you're fat!

Your ego obviously prefers the first option. That safe little bubble lets you feel good about yourself, even if you have the sneaking suspicion that you're meant for something greater. But you can't live off applause, and gold stars were only awesome as a kid. It's not enough to hear "well done," and the thrill of getting five stars doesn't last forever.

★ *Lesson* ★

Becoming exceptional means
making yourself vulnerable.

A few years ago, when I was coaching, I had a fabulous actress client, Amy De Bhrún, who is probably one of the hardest-working actors I know. We started working together because she wanted to move to the next level in her career, including getting paid enough that she could stop doing random non-acting jobs to pay the bills. Soon after starting with me, she was making a full-time living from acting. However, when she began to do more paid acting work, it was inevitable that she'd eventually get a bad review.

Her one-woman show got two wonderful reviews, followed by two "not so amazing" ones.

After feeling hurt initially, Amy wrote to me:

"I came to realize that the higher the level, the more open you are to criticism. There are more people seeing your work, and therefore there are more opinions, and you cannot please everyone 100 percent of the time.

So I guess if you spark a strong reaction in people, it is a beautiful thing – you have touched them in some way, and maybe enabled them to look at something within themselves… and from there, it is their choice whether they consider it a positive or a negative.

Once you can stand over your work and know you have given it 100 percent and for a greater purpose – that's the most important thing."

If Amy is going to continue being a successful actress, she can't expect everyone to love her. Well, unless she only performs for her parents and sisters, anyway. But she has bigger dreams than that, and you do, too.

Let's recap. Some people will think you suck no matter *what* you do. It's the truth. You'll never please those people who live off complaints and revel in other people's failures.

When I was growing up, my mother was a single parent; and for a couple of years, we lived in a subsidized housing estate, with a welfare allowance. The beauty about living in a low-income place like that is that everyone is equal. Everyone's houses were built exactly the same (literally the same house), and nobody had a lot of money or fancy cars. (This has changed now because of readily available credit, so you're just as likely to see a massive satellite dish and new car in poor neighborhoods). Now, I didn't go to fancy private schools, but because I was a voracious reader from an early age, I knew I was smart, and I had a good vocabulary.

I was at a friend's house in the neighborhood one day, eating fish and chips for dinner; and I asked politely if they had any condiments. My friend's parents laughed so hard. "*Do you mean* **tomato sauce**?" they asked, and then teased me for being so "fancy" for using the word "condiments." I was bewildered that an adult would make fun of a child for having a good vocabulary. It was the first time I realized that some people considered it "wrong" to be smart and different.

I was automatically considered "stuck-up" because I read books and I got good grades. "You think you're so smart!" my brother would always say to me, as if it were a bad thing to excel at school.

This is why criticism can hurt women so much. They think, *I'm just trying to do good in the world! Why would someone be so mean about it?* But people will. And for no reason, either. So you really can't worry about it.

You can try to make yourself small so that other people feel better about themselves. The truth, though, is that someone will always be threatened by any success – large or small – so why not go big?

Ditto with pricing. You can charge $10 an hour or $1,000. There will always be someone who will think your price is too expensive no matter *what* you charge, so why not charge what you like?

7. Good is good enough

I really should have called this book *Lazy Bitch*, because I'm all about finding the short-cuts to success, despite being a recovering perfectionist. I'm smart and lazy – a great combination! I have extremely high standards and love delivering good work, but at some point, I just have to accept that life can be easier if I chill out a bit and give up the guilt.

Being a perfectionist sets you up for constant disappointment and feelings of failure, because nothing is ever really good enough. Even when something wonderful happens, there's a niggling feeling that you didn't deserve it. You tell yourself, *Well, that was a **fluke**. It doesn't really count!*

I didn't even want to call myself a perfectionist because I wasn't perfect enough! I didn't deserve the title – I was ashamed to admit that I wasn't perfect.

Back in my consulting career, my team had a big job to deliver for the United Nations. I say "my team," but everyone on the project got called away to different jobs; so in the end it was just me. Then there was a miscommunication with the client, and our deadline was moved forward. So we had less than two weeks to deliver a full Corporate Social Responsibility manual and training program.

Guess who had to "make it happen?"

I loved being that person who'd just *get it done*, no matter what. I put in a superhuman effort, and melded time and space to finish the project on time. I got a massive amount of praise from my manager and the client. It was a huge effort, and I should have been enormously proud of myself.

But you know what? I've never looked at that manual since. Why?

I was too afraid to see a spelling mistake. It made me sick to look at all that work because I felt like it wasn't good enough.

How many times have you received a compliment about a job well done, and replied with, "Oh, it was nothing!" or felt like a fraud because it wasn't a 150 percent effort?

That reaction can completely ruin the satisfaction of the moment, and it sets you up for a lifetime of disappointment and frustration. It also tells the Universe that you'll never be happy, and that you don't deserve to feel contentment or pride. The message is always "not good enough."

Extreme perfectionism is self-hatred in disguise; and it only serves to make us feel bad about ourselves. High-achieving women, in particular, can get caught up in wanting everything done right – and causing themselves and the people around them constant anxiety and stress. For example:

✤ **Being a perfectionist around your body and diet** can lead to disordered eating, and being unhappy no matter your size.

✤ **Being a perfectionist around your relationship** sets you up for failure because nothing your partner does will ever truly please you.

✦ **Being a perfectionist employer** makes your employees afraid to experiment in case they get things wrong.

By far, though, the most dangerous side effect is that perfectionists punish themselves constantly. They deny themselves happiness until they jump over increasingly harder hurdles to prove they're "worth it." This effect includes wearing ill-fitting clothes until you're a perfect size, not showing your creative efforts to anyone because they're not ready "yet," and ignoring the guy who's perfect for you because he's not conventionally handsome and you're waiting for 100 percent perfection.

> *"For a long time now I have tried simply to write the best I can. Sometimes I have good luck and write better than I can."*
> ERNEST HEMINGWAY

I wanted to be a life coach before I even knew what that was, but do you know how long it took me to do it? Over ten years.

I felt like I had to be perfect in my own life, and that was *never* going to happen. I would have waited forever, unhappy with my life, but too paralyzed to do anything about it.

I completely resisted the calling to be a money mentor because I thought, *Who do I think I am? I'm not Suze Orman!* Even though I knew I had something to say and wanted to contribute to the conversation around women and money, I felt like I had to be perfect first or it wouldn't count.

Now, I love being a role model and Queen Lucky Bee, but I'm also a real person. I've learnt to forgive myself instantly for any mistakes I make, and to feel genuine pride when I do a good job. I'm okay with being flawed. It's not my job to be perfect for you. I'm here to role model a different way of life: easy, chilled, and abundant.

There's real freedom in deciding that you *are* good enough. And what happens then is that you get to decide that you can be totally who you are right now, *and* have the life you've always dreamed of. It's absolutely okay for life to be easy.

You have to believe that success won't "fix" anything. Your fundamental personality won't change at all. You might make different decisions about what you will and will not accept in your life, like having minimum standards for how you're treated, or what you'll wear. You might stop to celebrate your wins more deliberately to show the Universe you're ready for more. And you might also be more willing to do things that scare you now, because that's how you move toward the life you know is waiting for you.

But you'll still be the same quirky, loveable self you are now. Flaws and all.

It's totally not necessary for you to be perfect to manifest the life you dream about. In fact, insisting on perfection will hold you back, because it's virtually impossible. Accept yourself as you are, show the Universe that you deserve more, and it will deliver.

Every time.

8. Create your own karma

I don't believe we come into this world with accumulated negative karma that we're destined to repay. I do, however, strongly believe that we have lessons to learn, and that we'll always attract what we put out into the world.

If you believe that you're destined to suffer in this lifetime, then that's exactly what you'll attract – unless you decide to start afresh through forgiveness and self-love. Set yourself free in *this* lifetime and give yourself permission to be truly successful.

Wealth, contentment, love, and adventure are just as valid experiences as suffering and poverty are. You can choose which ones you want in this lifetime.

Nothing is set in stone.

> *"Be grateful for luck. Pay the thunder no mind – listen to the birds. And don't hate nobody."*
> Eubie Blake

Being a Lucky Bee has nothing to do with being a selfish bitch who's arrogant or thinks they're better than others. In fact, if you believe in karma, you'll quickly realize that living your dream life allows you to act in ways that increase your positive karma *even more*, such as doing good things for others and being a positive citizen of the world.

And even if you don't believe in karma, doing those things still feels good!

You don't have to wait until you're successful to be a generous philanthropist either! Even if you think you have "nothing to give," remember: start before you're ready. *Be the change you want to see in the world now* – not at some point in the future when you think you're ready.

Before I manifested the Honeymoon Testers' Trip, things in my life were gray and average. Remember I told you that I was living in London, commuting every day to a job I didn't like, and wondering when the hell my luck was going to turn around? About that time, I decided that I was going to start sending out positive energy to the people around me.

I sent miserable commuters waves of happy vibes. I would select a particularly sad or bored-looking person, and send them wishes such as a fantastic sex life, great adventure, or unexpected windfalls. I had so much fun creating these "love bombs" for other people; and it cheered me up to know that if I could wish good things for other people, I could accept them for myself.

✧ Action ✧

Send out some positive
vibes right now.

We know that everything in the world is made up of energy. And I mean *everything*, from your body to your computer, from the trees and grass to the dirt. We become a magnet for things that vibrate at the same frequency or the same energetic level as us. So if you can align yourself with positivity, you'll attract similar people and situations. They can't help it: their energy is the same as yours, and like energy attracts like energy.

Similarly, if you're feeling particularly negative, and you constantly act in self-destructive ways that show the Universe you're unaware and uncaring, you'll receive your negative karma very quickly.

You might ding your car, stub your toe, or meet someone who says something really mean to you; and you wonder, *Where the hell did that come from?* It's because again, your energy has attracted their energy.

It takes conscious effort to break the cycles of attracting these things, and unchain your energy from negative people or situations. *But it can be done.* You'll see a change when you consistently apply these positive principles into your life. Some people in your life will drift away, new people will appear, and you'll start to see your vibes (positive or negative) reflected in your real life.

I experienced a big change in my life when I stopped doing things that were kinda douchy. For example – my friends and I went through a stage where we thought it was funny to steal traffic signs to decorate our student apartment; or we'd dare each other to steal silly things like pepper shakers from restaurants. I once stole a bottle of champagne, and thought it was *sooo* funny. Nope, it really wasn't. It was bad karma.

In my first ever corporate job I had a bully for a boss, and I hated every second of being in the office. It was torture being cooped up in that cubicle all day. I started to rebel, and looked for a way to kick-start my entrepreneurial career on company time. Not only did I use company time, Internet, photocopying, and phone calls to play around with my business ideas, but on my last day in the job, I mailed a large packet of the company's stationery to myself. Genius, right? No, it was evil and petty (even though I thought it was *hilarious* at the time).

Instead of sucking it up and telling my bully boss "I quit!" it seemed easier to sit back and collect my paycheck while doing the minimum at work. I thought I was so clever, in fact, that I wanted to write a manual for being a "Parasite Entrepreneur" (written on company time of course)! I thought I had it all figured out.

But karma got me in the end. I was *never* successful at any of my side businesses – mainly because they weren't about being authentic to my skills and talents. Instead, they were just about making money – any way possible.

What changed? I realized that the energy I was putting out into the world didn't match what I wanted to get back. Now I see *everything* as a reflection of the energy I'm putting out. My whole life is a positive affirmation that I'm a lucky person. It's become a self-fulfilling prophecy. Luck creates more luck, courage creates more courage, and good feelings attract more good feelings.

Decide to be a reverse paranoid.

When I break a glass or a mirror, I don't say, "Oh no, seven years' bad luck!" or blame it on bad karma. I'm mildly annoyed, but I move on. In fact, I deliberately ignore most negative folk tales or superstitions. They don't serve me, so why bother?

Instead, I pick and choose my beliefs to serve my greater good. For example, when I see a rainbow, I take a moment to reflect on my good luck and thank the Universe profusely for blessing me with such good fortune. I look out for four-leafed clovers. I figure any little reminder of luck can't hurt.

I see them as reminders, though, not the secret to my success. I give myself permission to be lucky even without the presence of so-called "lucky charms." I know I deserve luck because I send so much good out into the world. You do, too.

The more people I tell about being lucky, the more people believe me. The more others reflect that back to me, the more I believe it myself. It's like two mirrors side by side. Where does one reflection stop and the other begin? Who knows?

If you're a happy, positive person, you'll continue to attract even more of those qualities into your life. If you're a miserable, mean, unhappy, and negative person, on the other hand, guess what? More is coming to you, but you can decide what you get.

That's karma in a nutshell.

9. Manifesting is a muscle

Some people seem effortlessly lucky, but the secret is that they're more experienced in goal setting and making specific requests of the Universe.

Deciding what we really want is not easy. Some of us have very, very little practice in this area. Our manifesting muscles are weak. We're indecisive about committing to what we want, because sometimes it's easier just to be passive and let life and circumstance happen to us.

For example, you might be ambitious, but *how often do you actually write down your goals?* You might want to "earn more" this year, but do you have an actual quantifiable goal in mind?

Just like working out, the more you work on manifesting, the better you'll get at it. There's no doubt that a daily practice of goal setting will change your life. When you see the results of what you can manifest, your belief will be stronger, and it will work more quickly next time. It's self-fulfilling.

Sometimes you'll be in that magical flow: you'll set an intention for something, and it will happen almost immediately. It's crazy when it happens, but it's true. If you don't make a regular practice of goal setting, visualizing, and consciously creating your life, though, it can feel *so hard* – just like when you go back to the gym after an indulgent holiday.

When you hear other people's manifesting success stories, do you feel a tiny bit jealous? Like they're blessed by the Universe and you're not?

There's no secret to manifesting, but it requires patience and constant vigilance that you're staying positive and in the right frame of mind. However, to start with, the Universe needs to know what to send you. That's why a regular practice of goal setting is non-negotiable.

Vague goal setting is like calling up your local pizza place and saying, "Please send me a pizza."

They'll ask, "What size and what toppings do you want?"

And you say, "Well, I think you probably know me by now. You know what my preferences are. Just send me what you think I'd like. Surprise me!"

That's exactly what we're doing all the time to the Universe. We're saying, "You know what? I just don't have the courage right now to make a decision on my dream career. So please just send me a job you think I'd like." Or, "You know what? I really don't like my husband. Universe, please make him disappear, but don't ask me to change anything. Please send me someone better."

Practice making decisions and telling the Universe exactly what you're playing for – the shape, color, size, and the exact juiciness you're after. With practice, you'll start receiving what you *ask* for, not just a vague approximation of what you want.

Lucky women know what they want and aren't afraid to ask for it – as simply as ordering their favorite coffee at Starbucks. It can be as complicated as you want, but it requires practice and bravery.

Soon it will be simple.

"Diligence is the mother of good luck."

<small>BENJAMIN FRANKLIN</small>

10. Luck is an inside game

Is luck an accident? Honestly, I rarely see any stories of luck that can't be broken down into the *real* behind-the-scenes story – usually one of persistence and hard work, with a little serendipity thrown in.

Outliers: The Story of Success, by Malcolm Gladwell, is a really fascinating insight into the secrets behind seemingly "inexplicable" success stories. He writes about people who seem gifted or outrageously talented. Gladwell takes one-in-a-million success stories, and demystifies their "lucky breaks." Obviously, as a student of luck myself, I found the book fascinating.

Here's one brilliant example: what do 70 percent of professional hockey players have in common? Being tall? Having an awesome goatee?

Actually, regardless of any other factor such as height or background, 70 percent of them were born in the first half of the year, with at least 40 percent born in the first quarter. *Why would that matter?* Does that mean that Aquarians and Pisceans are just born with a genius for hockey? Haha – hardly!

The simple and extremely genius answer is that it has nothing to do with luck – instead, it's something practical and obvious. Basically, the advantage of having a birthday so close to the age cut-off date of January 1st is that you'd be up to eleven months older than some of the other players in your age bracket when you first start playing. Being older means you'll have better coordination and skill (for example, the difference in coordination between five- and six-year-olds is significant).

Having this slight advantage from Day 1 means you're picked into better teams, which consequently gives you more practice at honing your skills and becoming a better player over time. Plus, the extra confidence of being your team's star player – even at a junior level – means you'll probably get more attention from your coach. And all those tiny advantages can really add up over time.

Then, every year you play, the advantage repeats itself, until you turn professional. Yes, of course natural talent plays a huge part, too, but the game is rigged from the start for kids who are born between January and March. Isn't that crazy? And fascinating! An accidental combination of your birth date and a love of hockey becomes a self-fulfilling prophecy.

Gladwell proposes that if countries such as Canada had two separate leagues, they'd have twice as many major league hockey players as they do now. How interesting! What can we can learn from this? And how can we "hack" our own successes, and find those tiny advantages that add up over time?

In the rest of this book, I want to show you how you can apply these luck principles to your business to increase your abundance, love yourself, and achieve amazing results in your business or career.

You've seen how a seemingly "lucky" and random event like Mark and I winning a competition with 30,000-to-1 odds can be deconstructed. I believe you can find the cheat in most situations, and completely rig the odds in your favor. Not to manifest an arbitrary thing like winning the lottery, but to find the short-cuts to achieve your biggest and wildest dreams.

If you're willing to apply yourself daily, have absolute commitment to your goals and dreams, and wish to achieve audacious success, it can *totally* be yours.

No exceptions.

> *"The golden opportunity you are seeking is in yourself. It is not in luck or chance; it is in yourself alone."*
>
> ORISON SWETT MARDEN

Are you ready? Put your hand on your heart and repeat after me:

"IT'S MY TIME, AND I'M READY FOR THE NEXT STEP."

Let's start with your business!

Chapter 4

Your Lucky Biz

*I*n my early twenties, when I was trying to find my passion and purpose, I worked for a few months as a telemarketer in a call-center. This was indeed a crappy and boring job – especially for someone like me, who values freedom above all else.

Within a couple of weeks, I was the number two salesperson in the company, even though I refused to make cold calls. I probably could have been number one without much more effort, but I decided to quit. I was just lucky, right? Either that or I was a naturally good salesperson?

Actually, it was none of the above. Instead, I completely rigged the system.

Here's the background. Our shift hours were 5 p.m. to 9 p.m. For four hours, we had to constantly make cold calls to people at home, usually while they were trying to have dinner with their families, to convince them to buy an Internet service that they didn't want. And of course, it got demoralizing to hear "no" over and over, especially when we just wanted to help people.

However. In amongst all the cold calls, we also got a couple of inbound calls during that time – and it was a *fight* to answer those calls as quickly as possible. Every inbound call was a warm lead, which meant a *much* higher probability that the caller would sign up. So, one evening, I decided to stay back an hour to see how many calls came in after quitting time.

When everyone else clocked off to go for drinks at 9 p.m., I stayed around and answered every single inbound call. It was usually someone who'd just seen an ad on TV, or had been on the company website. They were calling to ask a few questions and to sign up.

And guess who took those sign-ups? Me!

So that became my routine. I'd half-heartedly make cold calls for four hours (sometimes I even just pretended, or called my roommates). I'd *maybe* get one sign-up in all that time, but then I'd work that one extra hour. I wasn't paid for the extra time, but the commissions I made during it more than made up for it. Plus I got the recognition and reward for being a top salesperson.

★ Lesson ★

It's okay to take short-cuts.

I'm aware that this might not be considered strictly 100 percent ethical. In fact, it was totally cheating, right? After all, I'd been hired to cold-call people, hadn't I?

Well, actually, *no*. I'd been hired to *get sales* for the company, and I just became very creative about how I achieved that. The thing was that their preferred way was actually a colossal waste of time and energy. I quickly discovered their secret: it was probably cheaper to hire a bunch of young people like me to cold-call potential customers during dinnertime than it was to spend more money on advertising (or on a better product)!

Since becoming an entrepreneur, I've made it my mission to find the easiest and most direct route to achieving the results I want. Obviously, integrity is one of my values these days, but the principle remains the same.

It doesn't *have* to be hard.

You see, most traditional jobs are absolute crap. They're actually designed to create more work. And when you're stuck working nine-to-five for someone, it's hard to innovate and take the "easier path" because there's a huge amount of busywork.

The best part of working for yourself is that you can use your powers of manifestation to find the "cheat," and then create results that – to the outside eye – seem like luck.

> *"Success is simply a matter*
> *of luck. Ask any failure."*
> EARL WILSON

Lucky people work to their strengths

If you've ever struggled to find your purpose and passion, you'll know they can feel like slippery concepts. But I bet you already know what your purpose is deep down. In fact, most people who tell me that they have no idea of theirs are just blocking the answer, because it often feels like "cheating." Sometimes the right answer is the easiest and most obvious one. It's cheating the system again, but this time in a good way. Why make things difficult for yourself when you can do what comes most naturally to you?

But for some reason, women often second-guess themselves when it comes to finding their purpose. If it's too easy, it doesn't count. If it's too enjoyable for them, it feels like a fluke.

"Will anyone actually *pay* me for that?!" Yes, they will.

Your purpose is supposed to feel easy (not effortless, mind you, but easy) and enjoyable. And keep in mind that just because it's easy for you, that doesn't mean it's easy for everyone. That's why people will pay you to work in your flow.

But how do you find your purpose?

I spent my twenties desperately trying to find mine. I read countless books, such as Po Bronson's *What Should I Do With My Life?*, and took *far* too many personality tests, both on- and offline. However, the clues were always right in front of me. All I had to do was look to my childhood, and remember how:

✤ I forced myself to be on the debate team because I had a huge desire to do public speaking, even though it terrified me.

✤ One of my first jobs was doing crowd warmup for kids' shows.

✦ My favorite present *ever* was the electric typewriter I got for my ninth birthday.

✦ I ran hot-dog and cupcake stalls at school to pay for my dance school's trip to Disneyland. I sold chocolates in the teacher's lounge.

✦ I volunteered to start a dance club at school to get out of gym class.

✦ I was always starting new clubs and creative projects to make extra money (things like selling horse manure, and forging Kylie Minogue letters with my typewriter).

✦ When I was twelve, we moved into a house with a blackboard attached to the wall in my bedroom. I thought this was fantastic, and started giving lectures to my brother and cousin.

All these early experiences point to me being a leader, creator, entrepreneur, mentor, coach, speaker or writer. Looking back now, it's super-obvious.

And funnily enough, they're all exactly what I do now (and I make amazing money out of them, too). It took forever for me to make them into my career though.

I spent my twenties doing things that went *totally* against my grain. I worked as a statistical analyst for an accounting firm, behind the scenes as an event planner, and even as a website project manager. They were all jobs that were structured, repetitive, stifling, and *super-corporate*. I got bored within a few months.

I had the skill set to be an entrepreneur from an incredibly early age; but for the longest time, I only used those skills in a voluntary capacity, instead of pursuing them as a career.

Why? Because…

- Being an entrepreneur felt too easy and obvious as a "purpose," so I felt guilty for wanting it.

- My family "worked hard" for their money, doing unpleasant or physically demanding jobs, so it didn't feel like a "real job."

- I was waiting for someone to give me permission, or to "discover" me.

- I felt like these were "hobbies," and that I had to find something "real" to do as a job.

- I told myself I was too young to be taken seriously as a coach or speaker.

- It felt like cheating to make money out of something I really loved doing.

- I'd never seen anyone do these things as a real job (no role models).

- I didn't feel qualified enough.

- I didn't see any women being entrepreneurs, and the men in the personal development industry really intimidated me.

✤ It felt like "selling out" to make money from something I loved.

✤ I also didn't want to screw up something that was so important to me. If I tried and messed it up, I'd be devastated.

It sounds kind of dumb to write the reasons out like that, because they're so illogical and counterintuitive. I mean, wouldn't it be easier to make a career doing something you loved and that you were naturally good at? My excuses were so irrational, but I know I'm not alone in feeling that way.

The "hack" for developing a successful business is to work in your flow, and to find that intersection – or "sweet spot" – between what you love, what you're good at, and what people will pay you for. When you find this sweet spot, it truly feels like you've "hacked" your life.

Finding your true calling

It's easier said than done, though: most women seem to really resist their true calling, which makes following it much harder than it needs to be. So how do you find out yours?

✧ *Action* ✧

Journal - what did you
like to do as a child?

- ✤ What did you do as play?
- ✤ What do family stories say about what you were like as a kid?
- ✤ What did you tell people you wanted to do when you grew up?
- ✤ What were your favorite toys?
- ✤ What clubs did you get involved with?
- ✤ What did you volunteer for?
- ✤ What did teachers tell you about your strengths?
- ✤ What was your favorite thing to do at weekends?
- ✤ What did you hate to do?
- ✤ What jobs seemed like the most fun?

Journaling about these questions is a great start, but don't feel like your answers have to be literal. Maybe you loved playing with Barbies, but that doesn't mean that you have to be a doll manufacturer.

As a child, I thought that being a proper grown-up involved working in an office all day, wearing a suit with shoulder pads, and sitting at a desk in front of a typewriter (I'd never seen a computer). In other words, it involved having "a serious job."

That's exactly what I ended up with; and holy crap, those suits were itchy! Being a grown-up *sucked*.

Do you remember the early 90s movie *Don't Tell Mom the Babysitter's Dead*, starring Christina Applegate? Her character has to find a job to support her five siblings after the babysitter in charge dies while her mother is away. In one of those classic 90s fashion montage scenes, she suits up in her mom's wardrobe, fakes her age, and talks her way into a corporate position at a failing fashion house.

OMG – I was in heaven when I watched this. Pinstriped suits! Mid-heeled court shoes! A pocketbook!

It was a world away from my real life. My mother had lots of different low-waged jobs, like cleaning houses and hospital catering. She never wore a suit or a uniform. I never saw a man wear a suit either, except at a wedding; and in my town, even the guests didn't really dress up much. Most people wore cut-off jeans, t-shirts, and flip flops in summer, then just switched it up with jeans and sneakers in winter.

Corporate life seemed like a hugely satisfying and glamorous profession. It also seemed like the only way out of my small town. So I ignored my entrepreneurial calling, and instead did a business studies degree, specializing in marketing. My first "proper" job was working for a major accounting firm in London. The building had a besuited doorman who greeted you by name, complimentary coffee machines, and a well-stocked stationery room where I could collect as many highlighters and Post-its as I liked.

I had arrived!

I bought myself some cheap pinstriped suits; found some sensible, low-heeled boots; and even sported a pair of tortoiseshell glasses (pre-laser surgery). I felt like a proper businesswoman!

However, instead of feeling like an efficient, high-powered woman of the world, I quickly realized that I'd made a *huge* mistake.

Firstly, I was incredibly clueless about "office politics" and I naively assumed that if I worked hard, I'd be rewarded. I'd also never experienced sexism before, and the reality of it shocked me. When I left one day at 5:30 p.m. and saw my boss pointedly look at his watch, I realized that even if I found short-cuts to finish my work, I still had to sit there doing busywork to justify my position.

After my first month, I knew that I wasn't meant to be there; but I'd signed a year's contract. I was disappointed in myself for making such a monumental screw-up; but even then, in my misery, I never considered starting my own business. I figured that this was what life was about – hating your job. Weekends were for the enjoyable stuff.

I ended up being the biggest clock-watcher ever. I had moments of brilliance where I got my work done quickly, interspersed with miles of boredom when I had to sit at my desk until 6 p.m. because that's what everyone else did. I used to drop my pencil on the floor when my horrible mean boss walked past so I could hide under my desk. Even though I always met my deadlines, it wasn't with any sense of pride or pleasure. I was only in my early twenties but I could feel the life force draining out of me with every day.

Some people *do* love their jobs, but it's not the norm. A lot of people only tolerate their jobs because they think they have no choice about leaving. Some people loathe every second of their work, and that loathing spreads to every area of their life until it sucks every shred of happiness out of them. Remember: you attract more of what you feel! If you hate your job, your commute, and your boss, you'll end up in situations that generate more of that feeling. If you know that you were born to be an entrepreneur – what are you waiting for?

To be honest, if you hate your job, you shouldn't ask yourself *if* you should quit and do something else. The question is *when*. A bad job, complete with the boss from hell, can scar your confidence for years. Even a boring or mediocre job just gives you permission to live a boring or mediocre life.

While I initially felt somehow grown-up in my corporate job, experience soon showed that the other parts of corporate life – the meetings, the bureaucracy, and the lack of autonomy – just didn't suit me. Entrepreneurship, on the other hand, plays to my natural strengths.

That's *true* abundance – when you're in flow with what you do every day.

And guess what else? Playing to your strengths is an *ongoing process*. When I started my business, I had to keep tweaking further and further to find what I was really good at. Nothing's ever set in stone, and we have the ability to change our minds over and over again if something isn't working.

In fact, continuous tweaking is *necessary* if you want to create a Lucky Bee type of business where your talents meet the marketplace.

✧ Ask yourself ✧
Are you working to your
natural strengths?

Is what you do for a living aligned with your natural strengths? Or are you fighting against what you "should do"?

It's entirely possible to find the perfect fusion of your natural strengths and a business that people will pay you money to do. If your imagination can think it up, it can usually be monetized. Trust me.

In a coaching session, one Lucky Bee mentioned how she loved her job organizing holiday respite care for people with disabilities, but was increasingly frustrated about where she lived. She'd just come home to her beach town after two years of living in Canada, and was desperate to get back to the winter life. Her dream was to live near mountains; and although she'd never lived in Switzerland, something in her heart told her that was the place to go. She desired to quit everything and become a ski bum in Europe, but she was frustrated because saving the money was taking so long. She was worried about finding a job when the competition was so fierce, even for low-paid ski jobs; and part of her felt that it wasn't a "real job."

I suggested that she look at what was really important to her and how she could have both of these things in her life: the career she loved *and* the freedom and adventure she craved. I asked her if she realized there were organizations that arranged skiing holidays for disabled people.

She'd never thought about it because it just seemed too easy and obvious. But then she got excited. No more angst between career and "dream life" – the solution was perfect; and with her experience and personal passion, it shouldn't be too hard for her to find a job. She almost couldn't believe that it could come together so perfectly.

Why couldn't she come up with that solution herself? In hindsight, it was completely obvious, but she almost needed permission from someone else to live a life that was perfectly suited to her as a whole person. We're so used to separating our lives into segments: our passions versus the things we have to do for money. A perfect example is to take a totally normal job and combine it with a passion. Here are some cool real examples of people I've met recently:

❖ **A chaplain for motor-racing festivals.** Perfect. This guy could stay a "man of God," which is his higher calling; but combine it with a huge personal passion for racing motorbikes. You might wonder how this works, but within the motocross profession, there are a lot of injuries; and like any profession with a high injury rate, there are people who need counseling and support.

❖ **A hairdresser on a cruise ship.** Just because you have a traditional "bricks and mortar" type business, it doesn't mean you have to stay in one place. This lady combined her love of travel with her salon-based skill set. Alternatively, she could also have set up a mobile hairdressing service, and then niched down to find a customer base that she loved working with.

❖ **A bookkeeper for a private island.** As a bookkeeper, she has a "traditional" job, but she hated working in a traditional office, and craved more flexibility and adventure, especially once she had kids. So now she specializes in working with tiny, family-run private islands. Several times a year, she goes to stay in their resorts to do their reports and taxes. I suggested that she niche even further, and call her business "Island Accounts" or something. Use a palm tree as a logo!

And these are all examples of pretty traditional, "old school" jobs that have been around forever. Imagine what you could create in the "new world" economy where you can basically invent an entirely new career.

So many people believe that work isn't mean to be fun; and this assumption often crosses over into entrepreneurial life, too. In fact, there's a strong belief that "everyone hates their job," but that we have no choice because there are bills to pay! Hating your job is a part of life, right?

I've been told this many times by friends and well-meaning relatives. When the Honeymoon Testers' travel extravaganza finished, we were told with *barely* disguised glee, "Well, you'll have to go back to the real world now, won't you?" The implication was that we'd been living a fantasy life that would now have to become "normal" (aka crappy) again.

No way. We used our experience as motivation to *completely* change the way we lived, and ended up completely changing our lives for the better.

GUESS WHAT? THE REAL WORLD CAN BE AWESOME, TOO.

I'm not saying it's always easy to create a business that supports your dreams and passions. One major reason for this is guilt. After all, we're constantly told: "*Life isn't meant to be easy.*" You work, you pay your bills, and then you die.

Many Lucky Bees tell me about the guilt they feel over out-earning their parents, especially for work that comes easily to them. One Bee spoke of her dad getting up at dawn every day and working physically hard all day for minimum wage.

It therefore seemed almost obscene for her to make good money as a mindset coach. After all, she wasn't working with her hands or creating anything tangible. She was "only" talking to clients over the phone, so it felt *unseemly* somehow – as though she was doing something wrong, illegal or shifty. In fact, even the words "online business" often have an edge of "scam" for the older generation.

It *should* feel easy and enjoyable to make money; but doing so often comes with the guilty feelings of *Who am I to experience such good fortune?*

That's what we have to work to change!

I understand why this happens. I mentioned earlier that my own mother worked many jobs while I was growing up: as a cleaner, a secretary, a waitress, and in later life as an assistant nurse. She worked long hours with the sick, elderly, and profoundly physical disabled; and although she mostly liked her work, it took a lot out of her physically, mentally, and emotionally.

I was embarrassed to tell her that I could make her daily wage in one hour, and not by doing something that was hard or challenging for me either. It felt unfair, but I realized that I couldn't hold myself back any longer. Who did it serve for me to hate my job, too? Would it make her (or me) feel better if I resisted the easy and enjoyable way to make money?

If you embrace the path of least resistance, you'll probably have to get over the fact that you'll earn more than your parents, friends, and family; and for doing something that you love as well. I'm not saying that it's going to be easy, but the Lucky Bee way of life is to find the flow and learn to be okay with accepting abundance in exchange for your talents. And to be a role model for others.

✧ Ask yourself ✧
Are you unconsciously limiting your income to appease other people?

The very easiest way to have luck in your business or career is to do something that you love. I know: this can be an incredibly overused cliché. When I worked in one of my cubicle jobs, I remember reading the book *Do What You Love, the Money Will Follow* by Marsha Sinetar; and I was like, "But *when*, mofo?!"

The problem was that I'd completely misunderstood the mantra. Even in my early business ideas, I'd started doing things for money, or because I thought something was a good idea. I didn't start anything for the love of it. So the money *never* followed. My heart wasn't in it.

The problem isn't usually lack of ideas. It's not taking action on the *right* idea for *you*.

My first ever e-book was called *Internet Dating Tips for Men.* I wrote it because I was SICK of all the guys I met online who had *no clue* on how to best market themselves. I thought it would be fun to be a dating coach, but that idea quickly fizzled when I started dating Mark. To be honest though, I would have gotten sick of the topic within six months (which was coincidentally my attention span in my corporate career, too).

My next online business involved helping women to lose weight for their weddings with a raw food diet. I thought it was a good idea, I liked the name "Raw Brides," and thought it was an interesting niche. However, it was a problem *for me* for several reasons. Firstly, I'm not that into weddings (which is ironic, given that I've renewed my wedding vows eighty-seven times); and secondly, I'm not an expert in health… or weight loss… or raw food. In other words, it was an interesting idea – but not for me. Plus, say it out loud. Raw Brides. Lots of people were like "Rob Rides… what's that?"

★ *Lesson* ★

Just because you're good at
something, doesn't mean you
have to do it for a living if
your heart isn't in it.

I'm a pretty good event manager, and I excelled at several event management jobs, but I'm no longer passionate about working behind the scenes. It's all about working on stage and being the CEO for me now. I was also a great one-to-one coach, but I realized that my true strength was in teaching large groups instead.

Remember that no matter where you're at in your business journey, nothing is set in stone.

Keep refining and ask yourself, *Do I still enjoy this?*

★ Lesson ★

It's okay to evolve.

Trust me, you'll probably still resist making it easy. Even as you become more successful in your business, you're likely to keep trying to find the hard path. Sometimes you'll just do it to prove that you can. Other times, it will be because you feel guilty.

Example: how do you manage your email?

Usually, when you start out in business, you can be really available to everyone because you don't have much going on. Then, as your business grows, it can be hard to pull back from that. In my Bootcamp, I often hear, "But Denise, everyone deserves a personal response! I love responding to my emails personally."

I agree that connecting personally is great, but I also know that email is *not* the format for me. It actually makes me feel anxious and helpless to try to help people over email, so I decided to outsource that part of my business.

I'll answer questions on my public social media pages because it benefits my whole community. I'll also do occasional free live webinars, or help people in my paid Money Bootcamp. But no – I won't do email. (And I don't do private messages on social media either.)

Of course, you can do what you want, though. If you love answering email, keep doing it! However, be aware that email *can* create boundary issues.

For example:

✦ Maybe your clients email you too much to ask questions when they could Google the answers themselves.

✦ Maybe you've trained them to expect a five-minute response time.

✦ Maybe you spend hours crafting responses to help people with their individual problems, and they never even say thank you. (This one's especially problematic when you *know* that the answer to their question is actually to work with you further.)

✦ Maybe it's even a money block – a way to sabotage your time – so you can feel busy and lose yourself in your inbox, rather than doing money-making activities.

Does that sound harsh and mean?

Yes, I used to think so, too. But now that I've stopped answering my emails personally, I have so much creative freedom and energy. Having an assistant manage it for me means I usually have fewer than twenty emails in my inbox; and I simply couldn't run my business if I had to answer every email that came in myself.

Trust me: my customers are still well taken care of. Not by me personally, of course; but if you email Oprah's team, do you expect Oprah to answer you personally? I know I'm not Oprah, but you get the point.

I know we all want to be everything to everyone; but you have to remember that you serve in the way that works for you first. Also remember that your energy is a finite resource, but as you grow in business, your email will grow exponentially.

You've gotta do what works for you, so that you have the energy and creative space to actually create valuable content for your customers/fans/tribe. If you didn't have to deal with all that email, what would you be able do with that time?

I know that if I was responsible for our customer service inbox, then yes, I'd be able to respond to everyone individually; but I wouldn't be able to serve my whole community as effectively. It's one vs. many.

You could also have a fear that outsourcing your emails will make you unreachable and unapproachable. Yep, I've had that response!

I totally agree that I'm unreachable, and that's by design; but I'm definitely not unapproachable. I just have boundaries over *how* I give of myself. I always, always try to answer questions that I get asked on social media. I'm not perfect, but I'm sincere in serving the Lucky Bee community to the best of my ability.

But if someone sends an email? Nope. I'm definitely unapproachable!

I see other entrepreneurs say things like, "Email me, I read every response!" and I either think, *Bullshit!* or it stresses me out to even think about!

Sometimes I'll do an "Ask me Anything" post on social media. Inevitably, I'll get someone who asks to send me their question personally, and they get pissed when I say no. I'm happy to answer questions if it benefits everyone. Otherwise, nope.

Often the most powerful thing to do in business is to say "no" more often.

✧ *Action* ✧

Figure out what you're doing in your business that doesn't serve you. Make a plan to stop doing it!

It's weird, but we women often feel the need to punish ourselves by actively making things harder than they need to be. Sometimes, doing the admin or crappy jobs in your business is the hard path, but you resist giving it up. Yes, it's weird but it's true. And there's another common reason we do it too: fear.

For example, I'd been joyfully writing, speaking, mentoring, and creating from such a young age, but it took me a *long* time to make it my career. Why?

Because I was afraid.

This is probably the number one reason that you'll sabotage yourself and resist creating a successful business. It's because you're afraid: afraid of failure *and* afraid of success.

I was afraid of people telling me I was too young, too uneducated, from the wrong kind of background, too fat, or not pretty enough.

Doing what I love is really freaking awesome. I love helping women to be brave, do things that scare them, create businesses, and live inspired lives. But doing my own work *still* scares me. Yes, even now! There's no amount of money that completely makes the fear go away.

The good news is that things that scare you today won't scare you tomorrow. The bad news is that there's always something new to be scared of (because you're always growing and changing). But if you stick to your greater vision, there's nothing you can't get through.

After all, what's the alternative? Even being scared is much better than trying to fit into the mold of working for someone else!

And once you understand that *everyone* is scared, you'll stop seeing it as a barrier or a sign from the Universe, and start seeing it as more like an inevitable challenge to get through.

"A pound of pluck is worth a ton of luck."
James A. Garfield

Writing this book and *Get Rich, Lucky Bitch!* caused me many shuddering nervous breakdowns and tears. Writing my next book will probably create the same result. Business can be scary!

Why was it so scary? Even though I'd spent a lot of time writing for my website, I didn't think of myself as a "Proper Writer." Perhaps it was because I did Business Studies at University instead of becoming a journalist. If I didn't have a certificate, how could I call myself a writer? What a fraud!

And if you could have eavesdropped on my self-talk you wouldn't have believed I was a mindset coach: *What if the book is shit? What if people hate it? Oh, it's terrible. Nobody's going to buy it. I'm going to throw up if anyone does buy it.*

Just because I teach success doesn't mean that I'm immune to self-doubt and criticism. Basically every friend who's written a book has told me they felt the same way. And almost every famous author who's brave enough to admit it has talked about feeling the same, too. Apparently, it's the curse of creativity!

So how do you get past the fear? By doing the thing you're afraid of.

I got through my fear of writing a book by... writing a book! I got over my fear of asking for the sale by... asking for the sale. Repeatedly. Ditto with blogging, with sending out my newsletter, and with public speaking.

As Hugh Laurie says, *"It's a terrible thing in life to wait until you're ready."* In fact, there will never be a time when you magically feel *ready*. You have to do the things that scare you, move yourself through the fear, and prove to yourself that it's just a feeling: one that will keep you small and cramped in a life you don't love if you let it.

Everyone goes through fear. You're not alone. I constantly have to work on my feelings of fear because I'm always pushing myself to try something new. And all my successful business friends say exactly the same thing. I'm never complacent, even now, this far down the track.

★ Lesson ★

Fear means that you're
constantly growing.

I wish I could tell you there is a magic pill that makes everything awesome and fear-free, but it's not true. That's why most people stay in a job they hate rather than starting their own business: their fear is too great.

I know that you're different, though.

Want a few examples of other people who are different, too? I've included the stories of many examples of creative artists and entrepreneurs in this section, because I've noticed that all hell can break loose when we women go out of our comfort zones and really endeavor to earn money from our innate talents and abilities. Being in business can bring up all of your worst insecurities and fears about yourself – fears such as being broke and homeless, or losing all your friends.

So, even if you don't fit into any of the following categories, see what you can learn from the people I talk about… and then apply it to your own life.

Dancers, singers, and actors

I'm starting with performers because I was one for a long time. I started tap, jazz, and ballet lessons when I was eight; and I took to them really easily. I loved all of them; and soon I was dancing almost every day after school. I spent every weekend performing in local competitions and virtually anywhere our dance teacher could find a stage – local shopping centers, festivals, and retirement homes. She promoted us everywhere, and gave us such a great work ethic.

I never actively pursued professional dancing, though, because I was *convinced* that I was too short and had the wrong body type. You know who's the exact same height as me? Madonna.

I'm not saying that I was good enough to perform professionally, but who knows what I could have accomplished with the desire and hope I had? I'll never know, though, because I completely cut off any possibility with the belief that I was too short.

Contrast me with my friend Paul: a professional dancer who performed regularly on cruise ships and touring shows from age seventeen (he works behind the scenes now). What most people don't know about Paul is that he had a car accident when he was fourteen, which left him with severe leg injuries. He still has trouble fully pointing his toe, but he disguises it extremely well through good technique and hard work.

If you saw him bare-legged, you'd notice some scars and a slight limp when he's tired, but he was still an amazing performer. I've heard people say to Paul that he only worked regularly because he's a guy and he's good-looking. Trust me: Paul could have had a great excuse for not being a professional dancer. He's also extremely dedicated to his technique and physical appearance, which is imperative in his industry. Still, many of his dancer friends who didn't work as regularly probably pass Paul's career off as "luck." Paul, however, never thought of doing anything else. He just had no Plan B.

There are a lot of dance schools where I grew up, but not all of the most beautiful or talented dancers from those schools made it. Some did through sheer hard work and determination; and one of those local success stories is Joshua Horner. Everyone watching Josh at our dance competitions knew he was amazing, but there were others just as good who seemed destined to succeed and didn't.

Josh won a grant to attend the Australian Ballet School, and has danced in many productions like *Billy Elliot* and *Moving Out!* After working at Disneyland as a choreographer (his dream job), he got his big break as a judge on the Australian production of *Dancing with the Stars*.

Not bad for a local boy, and just "luck," right?

No way. Josh is one of the hardest-working and entrepreneurial creative people I've ever met. He's constantly starting new businesses and making his own opportunities. Why wait for the perfect audition when you can make your own luck?

Josh says, "People say to me, 'You're so lucky, Josh!' and I really want to slap them. I'm not lucky. I planted all these seeds, and I planned my career out. I really listened to what I wanted to do, and I never let anyone stop me."

There were plenty of talented dancers from our town who had the same opportunity and training as Josh, but *he's* the one who made it happen. He did it by auditioning, working on his craft, fixing up his skin with acne medication, networking like a mofo, making his own YouTube videos… and now he's created his own global online talent competition, *Dance Upon A Dream*.

Amy that I talked about earlier in the book? When the perfect parts weren't around, she created her own one-woman shows. I even played an extra in one of her web series once. She created her own opportunities to make money.

Nothing like that happens by accident.

You might not be a dancer or an actor but the same lessons apply to virtually any business. Are you waiting to be "discovered" as a public speaker, or are you making your own platform through the many outlets available to you?

★ *Lesson* ★

Your excuses for not living your
dreams are just that - excuses.

Have you got a story about why you're not allowed to be successful as a businesswoman? Some of the most common ones I've heard are:

❖ I have the wrong education.

❖ My accent isn't clear enough for me to do podcast interviews.

❖ I'm an introvert, so I can't do public speaking or put myself "out there."

❖ I'm not pretty or skinny enough for videos.

Yeah, they're all just BS excuses. When I was researching this section and finding out-of-the-box entrepreneurs, I remembered one of my dance colleagues who turned her "shortcomings" into an advantage.

Case study
The tiny dancer with a big dream

Meaghan Davies is an accomplished dancer, actor, singer, and voice-over artist. She's also extremely petite, at just under five feet tall. Here are her beautiful insights in her own words from an interview:

Have you had people (friends, family, teachers) tell you that you couldn't be a performer?

I had a dance teacher who made me feel as small as an ant. In a way, it made me more determined to prove myself. My parents encouraged me, and I don't ever remember them sitting me down and telling me to "get a real job."

How have you used your height to your advantage?

Anything that makes us different can be a weakness or a strength. It's usually a weakness if you listen to your detractors. However, if you have courage inside, you realize that your differences are what make you stand out from a crowd; and this knowledge can be quite powerful.

Being just under five foot has certainly lost me a lot of roles I'd be considered for if I were a few inches taller. Yet at the same time, it's helped some pretty incredible people remember me. I don't think that without all the other ingredients (persistence, talent, professionalism), my height would have helped me. But with these qualities, it has certainly given me my own little niche. (Note from Denise – for example, I saw Meaghan perform in an amazing children's musical where she convincingly played a twelve-year-old.)

Have you had any particular "lucky breaks" that you felt were divinely guided, or in the right place at the right time?

Absolutely. It is quite serendipitous when I look at how I got to work with a certain person. They might have seen me in a show that I almost didn't do. Or I was in the right city at the right time.

Not many lucky breaks come from just having your CV and headshots out there. Often when you think you've just had enough, you get a call from your agent for a job you are so excited to do. That's what keeps you going. It keeps you hanging in there. It reminds you of why you do what you do.

Do you struggle to get paid well for what you love?

There comes a time also when an actor needs to start treating their work like a business. The craft is an art. But to run any business, you need to get paid.

I think it's imperative that we don't undervalue ourselves. I have trained for many, many years to have the skills I have. I started dancing when I was three; I learnt several musical instruments, attended back-to-back dance classes, singing classes, acting classes, university, and took additional workshops around the world.

These skills make me the performer I am today. And actors are continually asked to work for deferred pay. When the project is great, and the team is inspiring, of course I'll consider it. However, sometimes you need to step back and ask, "Who is gaining here? Is this my personal project or someone else's? Is it me or is it them who should be taking the financial risk? Can I work for nothing, again?"

The answer is sometimes, "Okay." The answer is sometimes, "No."

The easiest way to achieve something is to stop just thinking about it, and actually get out there and do it.

Here's what I learned from Meaghan that any business owner can relate to:

❧ Niching is important. Who cares if you're not like everyone else? Use your difference to your advantage and stand out!

❧ Talent is important, but persistence is imperative, too. Nobody's waiting to discover you, so put yourself forward.

❧ You're not just getting paid for one client or one job. You're getting paid for the accumulation of your skills, experience, self-education, and years of hustle.

❧ It's okay to get paid doing something you love, even if you love it so much you'd do it for free.

Artists, crafters, and other creatives

The "starving artist" mentality is alive and well in our generation, just as it has persisted for centuries. What's the deal with that? Who decided that it's a "sell-out" to actually get paid for your contribution to the world?

Why should you bust your butt creating something amazing with your hands, and then *not* get paid for it?

Case study
Art and money

Business coach and art marketing consultant Freea L. Sarti helps visual artists to build sustainable businesses and actually make money from their art. She shares some thoughts on "luck" and artistic success.

With the artists you work with, what do you think differentiates those who "make it" and those who don't?

*The main determining factor in artists who "make it" is an artist's ability to allow their "creativity" to encompass all aspects of their career, not just when it comes to producing their work. They have a willingness to be flexible, to learn new skills, to do **whatever** is necessary to bring their dream to full fruition. This means taking **full** responsibility for their success, and taking full control of their future.*

By "making it," I mean that they can comfortably support themselves financially with their creative business; and in addition, that they feel a sense of life fulfilment due to their commitment to their own personal core values.

- *Specifically, they have the following attributes:*
- *They realize the importance of "investing" in themselves in terms of time, energy, and money.*
- *They know how to leverage their time, energy, and resources, so that they get the highest ROI (Return*

on Investment) when they're engaged in business activities.

- *They have a clear vision and strategic plan for following through.*

- *They work within the realm of their strengths, and work to improve or delegate their weaknesses.*

- *They're resourceful and persistent.*

- *They value themselves and their work or services.*

- *They're committed to integrity, courage, and perseverance.*

- *They're also fully committed to making a difference in their community, city or the world at large; and willing to storm the castle without hesitation.*

- *They move forward constantly, accepting that they **will** make mistakes. They also know that when they do, it is not a big deal, and that it will allow them to actually learn and expand like **never** before.*

How can artists overcome the "starving artist" mentality, and earn a decent wage for their work?

First, identify any limiting factors that hold you back from pricing your artwork fairly. If you are not sure what "fair" is, get help from a coach or consultant. (A really good consultant won't tell you what price to put on your work, but will help you to develop the skills and confidence to price your own work with integrity.)

Next, identify any limiting beliefs about money in general and financial success/comfort. Ask if any obstacles exist. If so, identify whether they are internal or external. Most are internal.

Now that you have a grasp on your constraints, develop necessary skills, acquire needed knowledge, and do any spiritual or psychological work needed to shift these constraints.

If you start working on other business endeavors first, without removing any obstacles in the way of you building a sustainable business and making a comfortable living, you'll waste precious energy and resources. Working through this process first will save you years of hard work.

Here's what I got out of this case study:

- Persistence again – it's just as important as talent.

- Nobody can tell you how to price your work. So stop looking for external validation.

- Inner work is important for virtually any career; so if you feel stuck, you have to do the work to overcome it.

Writers, coaches, and entrepreneurs

Ah – these are my people! If you're a writer, coach, or entrepreneur, every single piece of advice above for artists and performers relates to you, too. Oops, I hope you didn't skip those sections because you're not a dancer or artist yourself! *Every* creative profession puts you in danger of feeling vulnerable about your work. Almost *every* entrepreneur I've met has a touch of the "starving artist" about them, too. And virtually *every* woman I've met in business undercharges for her work or dismisses her own talents.

Forget about the voice in your head that says you can't make a real business – or a living – out of your innate skills and being *exactly who you are.*

The validation you long for isn't going to come from outside you. In fact, most people will probably tell you that you're crazy for wanting a different life. So if you make yourself vulnerable to other people's opinions, you'll probably never get started.

Lucky Bee Laura is almost twenty-six, and she's starting to do some coaching on the side of her job, with a view to one day making it a full-time vocation. She was totally deflated at a recent event because a much older woman told her that she didn't have enough life experience to be an effective coach.

Is that true? Should she wait until she's "old enough" by this person's standards? How old would that be… Thirty? Forty? Fifty? "Old enough" sounds like a moving target with totally arbitrary criteria. So, how does Laura know when she's had enough experience to quit her job and do it full-time?

It depends, doesn't it? Maybe she'll never feel "ready." Will anyone hire her if she's "too young?" Well – I firmly believe that you'll find the right clients for you exactly where you are. Chances are that the clients she'll attract will be the ones who will resonate with her particular skills and experience *right now*; and she'll be able to offer real value to them. If she waits until someone else validates her decision, though, she'll probably *never* be ready.

✧ Action ✧

Journal *your* excuses.

It doesn't matter what your excuses are: too young, too old, too fat, too… something. You're ready *now*; and nothing external will give you the validation that you're enough. Yes, you could wait until you're "perfect," but how long are you willing to delay your dream?

The exact same thing that Laura experienced actually happened to me several years ago; but it came from my *landlord* of all people. He was a man in his sixties, and pretty much the opposite of my ideal target market. As he showed us around the apartment, he asked me what I did for a living. When I said I was a life coach, his response was, "You're a bit too young for that, aren't you?"

My silent response was, *How old do I have to be?* But I felt ashamed and judged by him, even though, seriously – he would *never*, ever be a client, let alone someone I'd seek advice from.

Choose your mentors carefully. Not everyone is allowed (or qualified) to have an opinion on your chosen business.

So, if you're young or just starting out, should you wait until you've had more experience before you allow yourself to make money from your talent?

Well – how long do you want to wait?

I'd recommend starting *now*, even just on the side of your current job. Get the confidence you need through being in the trenches, even if you work for free initially (something you don't often hear me recommending, but I'll explain why below!). Start your apprenticeship now. That's how you'll get there. Not by dreaming or waiting for someone to give you permission.

The biggest reason for failure for aspiring entrepreneurs isn't lack of talent. It's giving up well before you can experience the success.

Every professional and entrepreneurial endeavor has an apprenticeship period where you may have to give your services away free or (sometimes *and*) take on other work to pay your bills. That's okay, and it's *not* failure. There's a learning curve in any profession, and it may take you hundreds of hours in unpaid grift before it pays off.

What if someone told you that you had to run one hundred practice coaching sessions before you got your first client? Maybe it's only ten. Maybe you have to write one hundred articles before one goes viral. Maybe you have to make one hundred videos before you can do one in a single take.

The problem is that there's no rule-book to tell you exactly what you need to do to complete your apprenticeship; and, sadly, most people give up well before they can start to taste some of the success.

Are you willing to keep going?

"Luck is tenacity of purpose."

ELBERT HUBBARD

JK Rowling's *Harry Potter* famously got rejected by twelve different publishers, but that's nothing. *Gone with the Wind*, by Margaret Mitchell, was rejected thirty-eight times! Would you have given up earlier than these women did?

Want to be a published author? How many manuscripts have you sent to potential publishers or agents in the *last six months*? None? A few, and then given up? Have you received and implemented any feedback about what you can improve about your book idea? Have you treated each rejection as one step in your apprenticeship... or have you given up, thinking that you're "unlucky" and that your work is no good?

What about self-publishing? Or are you waiting for external validation? I self-published my books at first, because I didn't want to wait until someone else told me that I was good enough. Since then, I've sold tens of thousands of those books; got a book deal eventually and my goal is now to sell a million copies. Nobody could stand in my way, certainly not a rejection from a publisher.

Luckily, Thomas Edison didn't take his repeated failures personally either. He was just trying to solve the problem of producing a workable light bulb; and the challenge was probably an incredibly exciting added plus for him. In the meantime, I'm sure he learnt a lot that he used for other inventions. Can you imagine if he'd said something like, "Oh, the Universe obviously doesn't want me to be successful. I should maybe get a proper job: this inventor stuff is too *hard*."

Nope, I bet he found it incredibly satisfying just trying to solve the problem – and he could tinker all day long without getting bored.

What if you could face your business in the same way? If you could play with it as if publishing a book or making a living from your website was a satisfyingly tricky problem to solve and nothing more – certainly not a reflection of your worth as a person! You'd definitely stop seeing the challenges and rejections you faced along the way as a sign to give up!

So seriously. Start. Even if you have to ease your way into it as a side job at first.

The ideal scenario for most people would be to make money out of their passion and creativity straight away. But having a day job is no excuse for not following your dreams now. Start on evenings and weekends, build your skills slowly, and one day you'll be able to charge for your services. Then keep going; and one day you'll be able to make a good, then a great living.

Think of it as your apprenticeship; and then eventually, you can graduate to full-time entrepreneurship!

> *"Luck consists largely of hanging*
> *on by your fingernails until*
> *things start to go your way."*
> AARON ALLSTON

Give yourself permission to create an amazing business from your skills and talents. Give yourself permission to dream. And remember that it's *never* too late to pursue your childhood dream. Don't wait.

Write.

Dance.

Create.

Sell.

Teach.

Inspire.

IT'S NEVER TOO LATE,
SO THERE ARE NO EXCUSES.

CHAPTER SUMMARY

❖ It's okay to choose ease and flow in your business, so choose the path of least resistance, even if it feels like "cheating."

❖ Work to your natural strengths. Money flows when you do what you love *and* what you're good at.

❖ Fear is a normal and inevitable part of business. The goal isn't the absence of fear – everyone has it.

❖ Don't let your excuses derail your dream of being successful in your chosen field.

Chapter 5

Abundantly Lucky
(Get Rich, Lucky Bitch)

A sk most people if they'd like to be wealthy, and they'll say, "Yes, of course!" I'm sure you'd give the same answer, right? I mean, who wouldn't? You've probably read books about money, and maybe you also have a regular affirmation about money and big money goals. So why aren't you as rich as you'd like to be? What's holding you back?

So much of the work I do now with my worldwide Lucky Bee community relates to money mindset. It's about how to change the patterns that we've grown up with or taken on board around money, so that abundance can find us more easily, and stay when it does.

But abundance doesn't happen by accident. We have to go through a process of releasing our money blocks and giving ourselves permission to be rich. Most of us are holding a lot of old blame, guilt, shame, and anger toward ourselves and others that we have to release so that we can become great money manifestors.

Obviously, I've now written an entire book – *Get Rich, Lucky Bitch!* – about money; and I highly recommend that you read it straight after this one.

What exactly are money blocks?

Some people have never even heard of the concept of money blocks before. Maybe you haven't either? Basically, money blocks are anything that holds you back from making the money you want.

You might think these blocks are forces outside your control, like:

✦ My boss won't give me a raise.

✦ The economy is bad right now.

✦ I'm already working hard – I don't have time to make more in my business.

✦ I can't increase my prices: my clients complain as it is!

✦ My husband won't let me invest any money in my business.

However, attracting abundance means going within to see where *you* are holding yourself back (i.e. "blocking" yourself) from making more money. This could include old stories and beliefs that you hold as true, past experiences that color your perception of your ability to make more money, or other energetic blocks that stop you receiving money.

And the tough, no-BS truth? These blocks are *your* responsibility to deal with, and nobody else's. That can be hard to hear but if you embrace it, then it can be empowering.

It's incredibly common for women to have massive resistance to earning good money; and we still earn much less than men in the entrepreneurial world where we set our own prices. Why? Why should we settle for less?

I believe we *all* have access to a river of abundance that flows all the time. It's just that some of us have rocks (okay, sometimes boulders – or even the occasional rusty car) in ours. There's still a trickle of abundance coming to us, but there's also a lot of crap in the way that slows it down – things like:

- ✦ **Negative self-beliefs:** Money is for other people, not for me. I'm not "destined" to be rich. My family has never been rich, so I won't be either.

- ✦ **Guilt:** It can't be so easy to make money. I should give my gifts away for free to the needy.

- ✦ **Negative thoughts:** Rich people are so selfish and destructive to the environment. Money is dirty and filthy. I don't want people to hate me.

In my experience, we female entrepreneurs find it difficult because we have to set our own prices, actually ask for the sale, and deal with our own taxes. These things tend to bring up a lot of fears, insecurity, and anxiety for even the smartest, most talented, and most ambitious women.

At one of my events, a woman told me that she abandoned her personal training business because she literally *could not* accept money from her clients. She loved what she did, found it fulfilling, and felt like she was making a real difference. However, it was making her broke, because every time a client tried to pay her, she went into awkward spasms and rejected it. Then, because she wasn't clear about her boundaries – e.g. insisting on payment up front or even on the day – clients just wouldn't pay her. They'd forget to bring money to training sessions, or even deliberately take advantage of her.

So this woman had to go back to working for someone else because she couldn't afford to run the business at a loss any more. It was very sad, especially since she loved it so much, and people were willing to pay her. That business should have been a no-brainer for her!

★ Lesson ★

Making money shouldn't
make you feel guilty.

Many creative women have incredible trouble earning money from their talent. That's especially true if they've made an unconventional career choice, or chosen something their parents don't understand. Sometimes that talent is so tied up in their individual identity that making money from it feels like cheating.

Plus, many women who now earn their living through a combination of services (such as coaching, speaking, and writing) start off providing information for free through blogs or by coaching part-time while working a full-time job. Making the transition from free to paid can feel like a leap too far.

Once they overcome that hurdle, they often start earning good money... but they usually find there's a limit to what they can make. I often ask my Lucky Bees, "What would be an *outrageous* amount of money for you to be paid?" We all have an unspoken and unacknowledged threshold – and earning anything over that threshold crosses the line and starts to feel weird energetically.

Money brings up *so many* emotions for people. When I first started out and shared how excited I was to be paid $500 for a speech, someone commented that I was being narcissistic and a show-off. What would happen if you got paid thousands for a speech? Or made money effortlessly? Who would that piss off? That's just one of the unspoken fears we deal with as women – fears that hold us back from earning more.

However, dealing with those fears and blocks allows us to move through the income thresholds we've been stuck in, and create the wealth that we want. That's really the *only* secret there is to becoming abundantly lucky with money.

Honestly – if you've read this book (and maybe *Get Rich, Lucky Bitch!*, too), you'll already know all the "secrets" to becoming a millionaire. You'll know that:

✦ You don't need to change who you are.

✦ You don't need to do anything differently.

✦ You don't need to suddenly become a "better" person.

What you *do* need to do is to maintain a positive mindset, and be very vigilant of your thoughts and feelings. I've found this is the most important thing in manifesting my own abundance, and it's what I teach my Lucky Bees in my Money Bootcamp now.

Oh – and this is life-long work. So don't beat yourself up if you're not "perfect" at it. I'm not either and I teach this stuff!

How do you know if you have money blocks?

Here are a few questions to ask yourself to see whether you have money blocks:

✦ Does money elude you?

✦ Does it slip through your fingers every month?

✦ Do you visualize yourself being rich and successful, but the Universe doesn't make it happen quickly enough (or at all)?

✦ If you're being honest, does money intimidate – or even scare – you?

It's really empowering to realize that *you* are the only thing that's holding you back. It's not someone else. It's not the Universe. And it's not your partner.

Let me acknowledge that it took me a while to take responsibility for myself. I didn't realize I had any money blocks because I was *always* reading books about money and I was *great* at affirming myself rich.

Buuut my bank account didn't agree.

Still, I didn't think *I* had anything to do with that. After all, surely my windfall was just around the corner? Sure, I was super-cheap with myself, and I had a lot of resentments toward rich people. But I still didn't think I could do anything about my financial situation beyond working harder.

At least, I didn't until one really interesting day where I couldn't deny the truth – that the way we handle money and abundance can show up in every part of our lives – any longer.

I was having a fabulous experiential coaching session with my then-coach, Corrina Gordon Barnes, in the local botanical gardens to discuss my goals for the following year. For each area of my life – relationship, home, health, and money – we found a different area of the park to represent what I wanted to achieve in that area. It was a hugely enlightening experience... until we got to my money.

We'd just finished "relationships" in the rose gardens, and I was eager to find my "money corner" in the park, and plan how much money I'd make in the upcoming year. I wanted to make a *lot*, even though my income had been stagnant for *years*.

"Where do you want to go?" asked Corrina. "Where's the best place in the park that represents your money?"

I spied a huge greenhouse on the other side of the park. I could see lush green plants inside. "My money is over there!" I said.

We were both full of enthusiasm as we marched toward the greenhouse, which was designed as a series of interconnecting rooms, each growing different types of plants. We walked into this gorgeous space, and I immediately saw a room full of tropical trees. It had quite a Zen feel to it, with smooth stones on the floor and a neat wooden bench.

"Okay, this is my money room. Let's go in there."

We stood outside for a moment, contemplating my money room. It was spacious, clean, and perfectly designed – a great choice! I put my hand on the door handle to enter the room… and discovered it was locked. For a second, I pressed my face against the window, and just looked longingly into the calm space within.

Oops, obviously my money wasn't in there!

We laughed and moved on. The next room that looked interesting was full of dark green plants and tropical flowers. This could represent my potential abundance nicely, too. We tried to enter, but it was the same story: the door was locked.

By this stage, I was getting a little annoyed. Corrina told me she'd been there dozens of times, and the rooms were *never* locked. What was this saying about my money goals?

I said to Corrina, "Maybe the Universe is trying to tell me something here." By that point, I just wanted to find a space and get on with it.

The next room wasn't particularly inspiring, but it was unlocked – hooray! I took a few minutes to walk around and get centered, and then we started to discuss my money goals for the next year.

Less than a minute into the conversation, a man entered the room. "You're not supposed to be in here," he said. "We're cleaning the rooms."

I couldn't believe it – I'd been kicked out of my money room! This was getting beyond a joke. Feeling like a naughty kid, I meekly left... and found myself in the very last room. I tried to laugh, but I actually wanted to cry.

And suddenly, I found myself letting it all out. I told Corrina all my fears about money. That everyone else had it except for me. That it was easy for other people to earn money, but not for me. That I wasn't allowed to be rich. That bad things happened if you had money. You get into trouble.

I'd always felt like there was a block between me and money; and there I was, brutally confronted with the evidence of my belief – a literal closed, locked door! I'd been shut out and then told off as though I was a little kid! I was so frustrated and disappointed with myself.

Suddenly, I noticed that the space we were standing in was beautiful. I heard rushing water, and saw ponds of goldfish (both lucky money symbols). The ceiling was huge; and the area was actually a lot more spacious than any of the rooms we'd seen before.

Once I'd calmed down, Corrina and I stood in front of the pond and discussed how I wanted money to show up in my life. I wanted to feel relaxed about it. I wanted it to flow effortlessly into my life and then be available so that I could spend it on things that I wanted: nice clothes, a beautiful house, great personal development courses, and donations to charity. Plus, I wanted to pay my bills easily and still have money left over for a healthy savings account.

I realized that it was hard to do all those things when my fundamental belief about money was that *I can't have it*. It didn't matter how much I visualized being rich, it was like putting clean clothes on top of dirty ones, or not showering for weeks and trying to cover up the smell with perfume! Nothing would change unless I changed how I *truly* felt about money; and it took physically standing in my "money room" in that park to realize that.

Little did I know what the Universe had in store for me after that: even more lessons about money! But my first lesson that day was that I had to go right back to the beginning, and examine my most basic beliefs. Could the message be any clearer?

✧ Action ✧

Reflect on your own basic money beliefs.

Specific questions you might want to reflect on include:

- ✤ How do your beliefs around money show up in your life?

- ✤ How would you describe your own money room?

✦ How do you treat money: do you hold on to it, hoard it, let it go freely, or let it pass you by?

You might think that the way you were raised determines your relationship with money, and makes it either good or bad. That might be true on some level; but you're an adult now. You're ready for something new, even if it means breaking generations of habits.

Interestingly, I asked the Lucky Bee community recently whether they'd grown up rich, poor, or middle-class.

The answers were *fascinating*, because there was absolutely no correlation between how much money they'd had growing up, and the health of their money mindset. Some Bees had grown up rich but had developed a terrible relationship with money. Others who'd grown up poor hadn't even known they were poor. What made the biggest difference was the way each Bee's parents had talked about money, which shows that perception is incredibly powerful when it comes to money mindset.

Clearing your money story will help you move past any negative money mindset you picked up from your parents.

My money story: rags to riches and back again

Growing up with a really young single mother on welfare didn't give me the best financial start in life; but honestly, I didn't think about it much. I didn't think we were particularly poor because I didn't know anything different, and as I mentioned, everyone I knew had the *exact* same house as us. My mother was eighteen when she had me; and my parents split up when I was two.

Money was tight, my mother worked several jobs to support us, and there wasn't a lot of extra cash to go around. However, like most kids, I wasn't too worried about money. I just wanted to play with my friends and have a good time. My mother's views on money were that it came and went, and that you had to work hard for it – but good fortune could also come when you least expected it. Mom is extremely lucky, and would often win at bingo or on the slot machines.

Then something happened when I was twelve that completely warped my view on money and abundance. Up until then, most of my friends came from single-parent families like mine, and many of those parents were unemployed.

When I was twelve, my mother met and married a very rich, older man; and we moved out of the estate and into his huge mansion. Everything changed, and it felt like we'd won the lottery!

Suddenly, we were being driven to school in a beautiful white car with pop-up headlights, instead of in Mom's old, brown wreck that had rips in the dashboard. I got a pony, and my brother got a motorbike. We had six cats, two dogs, and five acres of land to play in. A motherfucking pony. Like a proper rich girl.

It was *heaven*. We had a housekeeper, our own TV, and VHS in our rooms. I had a double canopy bed like a princess out of a 90s movie. Everything about that house was luxurious in that 90s way (intercoms in every room for example). There was a fully stocked bar in the rumpus room, a walk-in pantry, and closet, a three-car garage – to me, it was the ultimate house. Everyone thought we were so lucky!

My friends came over, and I loved showing them around our house, riding my pony Krystal, and hosting pool parties in the back yard. Every part of the house had something interesting to see. There was a giant Wurlitzer jukebox to play music, and a full-sized billiard table (my brother and I actually had professional lessons, like rich kids ha!). I had my thirteenth birthday party in that house, and I thought I was so cool.

I was the luckiest girl in the world!

However, as with so many people who marry for money and security, Mom and my step-dad quickly discovered that they weren't suited at all. And their big age gap only made it worse. Their relationship was often turbulent over the four years they were together. They would constantly break up, and we'd be kicked out "back into the gutter where we belonged" as my step-dad put it. Our little family moved in and out of that mansion four times, and each time we spent the periods in between in a different, small, cheap rental, which was all my mother could afford by herself.

It wasn't my mother's fault at all, and I never blamed her. But for the first time in my life, I understood the difference between rich and poor… and being poor felt shameful.

It was confusing and humiliating to tell my friends that we'd moved *yet again*, or that I'd had to cancel the next swimming party because we'd been kicked out of the big house. That experience taught me a very memorable lesson; but rather than seeing my mother as totally unbowed and determined, I made up a story that women were powerless because men were ruthless and owned all the power. I decided that I couldn't trust men *or* money; and for years, I told myself that if anything good happened in my life, it was just a matter of time until it all turned to crap. I remember thinking things like, *Don't get too comfortable*, *Good times don't last*, and *Rich men rule the world*.

And that mindset stayed with me for years.

✧ *Action* ✧

Write down your money story.

What's *your* money story? Write out your story like I did above, and see what patterns emerge from your childhood and early life. You'll realize that most of your current beliefs around money stem from one or two symbolic memories.

Once you identify your main money belief, you become free to choose something different for yourself.

Here are just a few of the most common beliefs…

"Work hard to make money… or it doesn't count"

I spent my twenties thoroughly exhausting myself by trying to prove that I could be independent and never again be at the mercy of someone else (like my step-dad). As well as going to university full-time, I always juggled four or five jobs at any given time. I wasn't a party girl, and college definitely wasn't the best time in my life because I was always working, terrified I'd run out of money.

I always saw a long weekend as a great opportunity to work more. But I never got ahead. I never saved – I always worked from paycheck to paycheck and worried constantly about money.

If working hard was enough, more people would be rolling in riches; and teachers and nurses would get paid as much as investment bankers.

Of course, that's not the case; but many women have still internalized the message that you can only make money if you work really, really hard. And they seem to hold that belief regardless of how much their parents made. I've heard it from women whose parents were incredibly successful (for example, doctors or lawyers), and from women whose parents were blue-collar workers.

Is that an old family story for you?

If so, it's time to break the link and allow yourself to make money easily from your skills and talents, instead of burning out!

"Overworked and underpaid"

Many women entrepreneurs undersell themselves and really *struggle* to charge well for their services. This pattern definitely starts young. Think about times where you've been underpaid or ripped off by employers. Your early work experience is usually rich ground for finding money memories that have shaped your current beliefs.

Because my mother had me so early, she couldn't get any qualifications until much later in life. That meant she was constantly working hard, and I didn't know anything different. From these early experiences, I internalized the story that you had to work hard (often with your hands or doing hard, physical labor) for money, and you got paid badly for it.

I've had many jobs in my life: over fifty at the last count. Many of them were low-skilled and low-waged, e.g. cleaning, waitressing, temping, or TV extra work. And they were mostly jobs that I absolutely hated.

I also did many things for money that I now regret. To pay for my school fees one semester, I participated in a paid medical experiment that involved testing a new morphine-based drug. Weeks after my experiment and long after the money was spent, there was an experiment in another hospital that went fatally wrong. Several people died as a result. But in my mind, what I'd done was justified. How else could I earn large chunks of money?

I also worked for an adult chat line company during university. That was, in many ways, the perfect job for me. The company was open twenty-four hours a day, so I could take on as many shifts as I wanted. It was a well-run office that looked like a marketing or HR firm, and the other women were all ages and ethnicities. I was nineteen, and I thought it was hilarious. I thought it gave me something interesting and memorable to tell people. Faking "sexy" moans at 3 a.m. while I was simultaneously studying for my economics exam was proof to myself that I was independent, and I was proud of it.

I understand why I did it at the time, and how I justified it to myself, but I'm sad that I didn't believe I could use my talents in better ways for a paycheck.

When you do something that feels "icky" to you for money, you'll never really prosper because all of your energy is against you.

Even as I progressed in my career, I never made more than a certain amount. My income threshold was stuck. Every time I was in line for a pay increase, I'd sabotage myself by either leaving the company, or feeling resentful that someone else was getting paid more than me. Simply having a money conversation was scary to me.

When I started my business, I had the *exact* same problem. I felt like I had to work with any client who came along, and that I had to accommodate their every wish even if it stressed me out. I can remember waking up at 4:30 a.m. for my international clients, or letting them text me whenever they wanted.

Plus, I also felt guilty if I wasn't working hard, so I resisted increasing my prices or creating passive income products because that felt like "cheating."

If I got really honest with myself, I'd have acknowledged that underneath all of this was the belief that becoming wealthy just didn't apply to me. For all my affirmations, I didn't really believe deep down that a welfare girl born to a teen mom "deserved" to be successful.

I had this belief that I'd be a completely different person once I became a millionaire. I'd be thinner. I'd definitely be way more disciplined and organized. I'd probably meditate every day. I'd wear fancy clothes all the time. I'd always be well groomed, and I'd generally live a very fancy life.

I was almost denying myself the chance to become wealthy, because "wealthy" meant all the things that I really – at heart – just wasn't.

I've *never* been someone who likes to wear fancy clothes. I regularly go out without makeup on. I live a casual kind of chillpreneur lifestyle – now. But because back then I had those thoughts in my mind about who a millionaire had to be, I created a huge barrier between where I was then, and where I wanted to be. I felt like I had to shift into another dimension before I was allowed to be wealthy.

Wealth was for "other people," not for me!

✧ Action ✧

Write down what being a wealthy woman means to you.

Ask yourself questions like:

- ✤ Do you have excuses about what you're allowed to earn?

- ✤ Do you have preconceived notions about how much someone from your background can make?

- ✤ Do you think you have to completely change how you dress or even who you are as a person if you become wealthy?

✤ Do you feel like you have to become a better person before you deserve to be a millionaire?

If you really examine your beliefs, you'll probably realize that you're holding yourself back because you know you're just never going to be that person. Maybe deep down you don't even *want* to be that person.

Identifying your story is the key to letting it go. If you want to delve further into this money stuff – make sure you check out my other book, *Get Rich, Lucky Bitch!*, or come over and join our Lucky Bee community.

We show the Universe how to treat us

Many women I meet say they want to be wealthy, but they're completely unwilling to treat themselves – even in the smallest way – as wealthy women. They wait for the money to show up before they even consider changing anything in their lives.

And I was no exception. Although I went to seminar after seminar about developing a millionaire mindset, in reality I felt guilty spending even the smallest scrap of money on myself. My daily actions were much louder than my "mindset."

I only shopped at second-hand shops, so my clothes always fitted badly. Even though I could afford new clothes (maybe not from expensive shops, but new all the same), I treated myself like a second-class citizen. It wasn't just money either: I didn't allow myself to wear my favorite perfume or take time to do my makeup. I didn't change my sheets or towels regularly, and I sabotaged myself in hundreds of small ways.

I read books about millionaires and dreamed about having a lot of money, but I lived like a pauper. Why? Because I felt like abundance was something that was going to happen *to me* one day, not something that I could manifest for myself.

I was waiting for my magical windfall, but the message I was sending out was "I don't deserve anything." And nothing is exactly what I got in return.

Time to grow up

Do you want your business to be successful, but you treat it like a hobby? What are you waiting for before you change that?

When I started my own business, I was very comfortable talking about becoming a millionaire "one day," but I was terrified to talk to an accountant. I literally sweated every time I went near a tax office.

Usually, when you have an extreme reaction to something, it's an indicator that you have a money block to clear. My (male) accountant reminded me of my step-dad, so being around him triggered my old response about men having all the power. Clearing that story allowed me to build a great finance team around me, without being scared I was going to get ripped off or abused.

Then, during the first few years of my business, I was terrified about paying taxes. I swung between being extremely cheap with myself (for example, using a really old, crappy laptop), and spending big chunks of money on courses that I never finished.

It can take time to release those old money stories – maybe that you're not good with finances, or that paying tax is scary.

However, it's *so* empowering when you finally allow yourself to be a "grown-up" around money. When you spend money wisely. When you have a good relationship with your finances. When you believe that's it okay to earn awesome money. Being a financial grown-up is a balancing act between the mindset and practicality; and truly wealthy women need both a good mindset and the practical actions to make what they want happen.

Again, it's not your goals but your actual actions that make a difference.

✧ *Action* ✧

Write down the money messages *you* are sending to the Universe.

Appreciate what you have

Just before we won the Honeymoon Testers' competition, I had a lot of debt and no money in the bank. Somehow, though, every time I wanted something, it would appear as if by magic.

For example, I manifested a scholarship for my life coaching course totally out of the blue, a publishing course at a lucky door prize, a ticket to an amazing conference I wanted to attend in Vegas, and lots of other small wins. I wanted to buy the Robert Kiyosaki *Cashflow* game and someone gifted me a copy at a trade fair. I was conflicted: frustrated that I couldn't earn very much money, while at the same time, appreciating that the Universe was providing me with the things that I asked for. I was lucky, but I was also *broke*.

Finally, I realized what was happening. The Universe was giving me exactly what I was asking for, despite me having such huge money blocks. I was getting results because I practiced the *feeling* of having the things I wanted in my life, rather than focusing on their lack. I got excited about travel and going to seminars, rather than telling myself I didn't deserve them. I aligned the opportunities to me, and they were attracted to my energy. We were a vibrational match!

It was awesome being such a great manifestor, but I also felt like a pampered child: getting what I wanted, but not experiencing the "adult" feeling of being able to pay for things myself.

Finally I said out loud, "Thank you so much Universe for bringing me what I want and need. I appreciate being so looked after. I'm a big girl now, though, and I'd like the opportunity to earn some actual money, so I can pay for things, too."

After that, some amazing things started to happen. Clients started showing up, and I allowed myself to accept actual money for my work. I deepened my research into money blocks and learned to be not just lucky, but wealthy as well!

★ Lesson ★

Appreciating what you have
will attune the Universe
to send you more.

A lucky windfall won't solve your money problems

Lottery winners almost never have their problems solved overnight by their unexpected windfall. Why? Because money doesn't change you: it only enhances who you already are. If you fundamentally believe that being rich makes you a bad person, or if you think that becoming rich will solve all of your problems, it doesn't matter how much money you get. You won't keep it.

According to NSW Lotteries, the odds of choosing all six winning numbers are approximately 8,145,060 to one, but here are some interesting statistics for you. Camelot Group (which operates the UK lottery) released a survey of their national lottery winners which showed the effect that winning the lottery had on each winner's overall happiness and lifestyle.

- 55 percent are happier after winning, 43 percent report no change, and 2 percent are less happy.

- 90 percent of winners who already had a best friend before winning are still best friends with the same person.

✤ 84 percent of winners have not taken up any new hobbies since their win.

✤ 32 percent of all winners have gained weight since their win, compared to 14 percent who lost it.

✤ 44 percent of winnings were spent after five years.

✤ 88 percent of lottery winners still participate in the lottery every week, and just 2 percent have stopped playing altogether.

What that tells me is that money, in itself, doesn't really change your life too much. If you struggled to lose weight before you were rich, you won't change your behavior afterward. If you don't know how to handle money, you will always end up broke.

You won't believe how many people tell me their number one goal is to win the lottery, and many people find my website every day by Googling variations of "How can I win lotto?" or "Can I use the Law of Attraction to win the lottery?"

This always ramps up – and my traffic goes wild – whenever there's a huge lottery jackpot! It's mostly spammers, but it's still interesting how many people see a lottery win as the only way they can become rich.

Yes, you can attract absolutely anything you want, *including* money. However, I honestly believe that focusing on winning the lottery as your *only* wealth strategy is a complete waste of your time. I actually don't even play anymore, because I think there are *much* easier ways to make money!

You might wonder, *Really? What's easier than being handed millions of dollars?!*

Honestly – making my own money has not only been incredibly empowering, but it's also something that I can 100 percent control myself. Putting all your hopes on winning the lottery, on the other hand, is a waste of your manifesting ability – and it could hold you back from creating your dream life now. I'm not saying that a lottery win isn't possible, but the commitment and obsession it would take is better spent on something you really want (and something that has better odds).

For a start: are you dreaming harder than everyone else in the modern world who also wants to win that lottery? Do you spend every waking moment vibrating and aligning yourself to a one-in-a-million opportunity?

Whew, that sounds like a lot of hard work! And what do you do the rest of the time? It's so much more fun to visualize your ideal day, your ideal house, your ideal partner – and you don't need a lottery win to manifest *any* of that.

Plus, the other problem with consciously trying to manifest a massive lottery win is that it often comes with a lot of need and desperate energy. There's almost always a hint of: "Puh-leeease, Universe! Give me a million dollars? It will solve *all* my problems!"

I've done this myself. I've bought a ticket and then watched the balls come down, trying to *will* them to be my numbers. But there's nothing I can do except buy a ticket. Winning is just a hope with no forward motion. There's nothing for the Universe to co-create with you. Action is a *huge* part of manifesting (second only to a big intention), but you can't take action to win a lottery other than to buy more tickets.

★ Lesson ★

Winning the lottery isn't the
solution to all your problems.

Don't be attached to HOW you make money

The one good thing about wanting to attract a lottery win is that you get excited about how you'd spend the money. You know: the multi-million-dollar beach house, private jets, holidays for you and your family, paying off debt, etc. But you don't need to win a lottery for those. I've been able to buy all these things (well, minus the private jet) with my own money. I didn't have to chance an arbitrary win for them.

Instead of dreaming of winning, channel that energy and excitement into writing down your goals (something most people never do), updating your dream board, and visualizing yourself living that dream life.

Just don't assume that a lottery is the only thing that can get you there!

What's holding you back from more money?

Have you ever thought about what's holding you back from being truly rich?

You might think, *Nothing! I'm ready for more money – bring it on!* If so, I want you to think deeper, because this reflection is hugely valuable.

Personally, I've identified many reasons that I'm not energetically aligned to winning money through a lottery. These include potential downsides like fighting with my family over money, and attracting unwanted attention. Not to mention the guilt I'd feel about winning money when I *know* I could earn it myself by simply becoming a better entrepreneur. I definitely am not manifesting a lottery win (as I mentioned, I don't even play).

If you lived for a million years, you'd maybe be able to align yourself to a lottery win by identifying and decluttering all the energetic blocks. And it could *literally* take that long for the Universe to engineer a win, given how much the odds are against you.

You definitely have more chance of becoming a millionaire as a businesswoman than you do of winning the lottery.

✧ *Action* ✧

Clear your money blocks to receiving
large sums of money. Start by
thinking of any downsides to having
a lot of money and being rich.

Let's play along with this question for a second. What downsides of winning the lottery can you think of? Before you say that I'm just being a negative Nancy for no reason, I want you to know that there's a massive amount of value in digging deeper.

Your energetic blocks around manifesting a lottery win are probably the same ones preventing you from that next leap in success right now. They're keeping you from doing things like attracting a few more clients, increasing your prices by 10 percent, or simply charging more for your services. Ask yourself...

✤ Would you feel guilty if you suddenly received a lot of money that you didn't have to work hard for?

✤ Would you feel like you're "cheating" if success just fell into your lap?

✤ Would you worry that you'd feel pressured to support your family, including the dead-beat members?

✤ Do you stress about having a massive tax bill?

✤ Do you have a sneaking suspicion that you'd waste the money and end up broke?

✤ What's the *absolute* worst thing that could happen if you won the lottery?

Now, before you get all depressed about your answers, let me tell you the fabulous news. You can manifest *anything* you want. But waiting for a lottery win is a great excuse for not simply deciding to live the life you want now.

Remember: you don't really need to win the lottery

I love author Tim Ferriss's take on the whole lottery win thing. In his best-selling book *The 4-Hour Work Week*, he says, "People don't want to be millionaires – they want to experience what they believe only millions can buy… a million in the bank isn't the fantasy. The fantasy is the lifestyle of complete freedom it supposedly allows."

Good point, Tim. Do you want to make a million dollars because that's how much your lifestyle really costs? Probably not. For example:

❖ Your first goal might be just to buy freedom from your job, and I'm guessing that you don't currently earn a million dollars in salary?

❖ Your next goal might be to buy a new car, and I'm guessing it costs less than a million bucks for your dream car?

❖ You might want to buy a million-dollar house, but remember, it doesn't cost you a million dollars to buy. Go see a mortgage broker and see how much you actually need as a down payment, and what your monthly repayments would be.

How to make a million dollars

You might think, *Well, I only need **one** ticket to win the lottery!* but again, I'll say, "There are easier ways to make money!" You only need *one* idea to make a million dollars, too. I've made more than a million out of one course alone.

To make a million dollars, you could:

+ Sell 100,000 e-books of $10 each.

+ Sell 10,000 courses of $100 each.

+ Sell 1,000 packages of $1,000 each.

+ Sell 100 packages of $10,000 each.

+ Sell 10 packages of $100,000 each.

There are *many* ways that you can create the life of your dreams. You can earn more money, you can start a business that supports your lifestyle, you could win the money, make it, hustle for it, inherit it… or thousands of other ways.

And the lottery has the worst odds out of all of them.

Anyone who's built a large fortune from scratch will tell you that it took time and effort to build long-lasting wealth. But is that enough? What about women who arguably had the same opportunities for making money?

Elizabeth Taylor was famously the first woman to make one million dollars for a film role; and according to reports, she grew her fortune to close to one billion dollars, despite not starring in a movie since 1994 (and that was *The Flintstones*)!

Liz's White Diamonds perfume made close to $70 million in 2010 alone; and her jewelry collection was worth more than $150 million at the time of her death. She had no trouble holding on to her wealth, and obviously invested well.

Contrast that to other film stars who ended their final years in poverty after having squandered their entire fortunes. Marilyn Monroe was just as famous as Elizabeth Taylor. Granted, she was only thirty-six at the time of her death, but even so, she left very little in her will besides her house, clothes, and personal effects. Would she have been able to amass a large personal fortune if she'd lived longer? Or would she have continued the same patterns of living month to month throughout the rest of her life?

It's not easy to change those ingrained behaviors, but it's not impossible if you're willing to completely rewrite your internal programming. That's exactly what I help women like you to do in my books and my Money Bootcamp.

Moneywise – would you rather be a Liz or a Marilyn? You can choose to change your financial destiny, and it's never too late.

Don't automatically believe what you're told about wealth

Clear your stories around what the media and movies have shown you about how millionaires behave. Movies (and society) have repeatedly shown us that very successful women are bitchy, manipulative, obsessed with high fashion, and a bit evil.

I had to clear all that stuff before I gave myself permission to be rich, because I didn't want to be evil. I didn't want to be greedy. I didn't want to be any of those things.

And you don't have to be either.

It's really important to clear your stories around all of this; and allow yourself to be wealthy *your* way. Give yourself permission to be exactly who you are *and* be wealthy at the same time. A lot of women think they have to give up some of their true self to be worthy of wealth.

However, giving yourself permission to be who you *really* are *and* be rich is incredibly powerful. You can be rich in whatever way works best for you:

❖ Rich and environmentally friendly

❖ Rich and philanthropic

❖ Rich and wearing flip flops

❖ Rich and happy

What kind of rich woman do *you* want to be?

Are you really serious about becoming rich (no matter HOW it shows up?)

Another reason to avoid getting set on a lottery win (or any other kind of windfall) is the assumption that it's the *only* way money can come into your life. Would you really be bummed out if the money came from other sources?

There are literally *no limits* to the different ways that money could show up in your life… but opening yourself up to them means you need to show the Universe you're serious about being rich.

Here are a few things you can do to show the Universe that you really are serious:

❖ First up, read my book *Get Rich, Lucky Bitch!*, and then join my Money Bootcamp. The Bootcamp is an amazing community of women, many of whom have completely changed their relationship with money and many now have six- and seven-figure businesses.

❖ Next, get really clear on how much you want to earn, and what you'd spend it on. You might not need as much as you think to feel rich. Don't make it the ever-increasing hurdle where you *never* feel happy.

❖ Clean up your money habits and prove that you can take care of what you've already got. That includes paying your taxes on time (and not fudging them), paying your debts, and tracking where your money goes.

❖ Get really grateful for your current life. Treat your current car as lovingly as you will your new luxury car.

❖ Use your income goal as your password, so you type it multiple times a day.

Put "Millionaire" after your partner's name in your mobile, so that when they call you, you'll be like "Yes!"

Lastly, constantly visualize yourself as a rich person. Think about how good it will be when you have millions in the bank, and visualize exactly what you'd do with them. Do this over and over again until it becomes normal for you.

You may find that when you do these things, good luck starts to manifest in your life. You may win a lucky door prize, or free tickets to the cinema at the start, even if the actual money is slow to come in. Keep track of all these wins and be grateful for your good fortune. Know that more is on the way.

In the meantime, don't put your life on hold until you get that big win. Buy a ticket to your success in other areas of your life – send the book proposal, ask for a pay increase, book the dream holiday, and love your spouse now. Don't wait to be happy. Don't wait to feel wealthy.

Money only exaggerates who you already are. Prove to the Universe that you are a happy and prosperous person now, keep working on your money blocks, and you'll be surprised about the good fortune that you'll allow into your life.

CHAPTER SUMMARY

❖ Money blocks are anything that holds you back from making money – and everyone has them!

❖ Your upbringing has a massive effect on your beliefs about money. It doesn't matter if you grew up rich or poor: uncovering your money story is the first step to clearing your money blocks.

❖ A lucky windfall won't solve your money problems, and you don't need to win the lottery to change your financial future.

❖ You can start feeling rich *now*. Don't wait – give yourself permission to be rich in any way you want.

Chapter 6

Self-love Will Change Your Fortune

*H*ere's a confession: I'm not a skinny chick.

I have ample hips and thighs; a cuddly tummy; and cute, plump arms. And you know what? I've learned to deeply and completely accept myself – not *anyway*; and not *in spite* of these flaws; but accept myself, period.

I'm a huge fan of the "love yourself" movement because I've come to understand that the most powerful component in manifesting your ideal life is deep love and acceptance. Years ago, I would have said that I have *enormous* hips and thighs, a *disgusting* tummy, and *flabby* arms; but now I know the power of language.

You can't hate yourself skinny, and you certainly can't hate yourself rich or happy. Trust me: I've tried that and it didn't work. I used to think that if I wasn't super-critical and hard on myself, I wouldn't be motivated to try harder. But that's not true.

Real, deep transformation can't come from a negative place. Ever.

I used to think that I didn't *deserve* to be successful or happy unless I was skinny. I used it as an excuse to not put myself up for speaking gigs or do videos for my blog. I kept waiting for the *some day* when I was allowed to be visible. The day when the person I was on the outside deserved the success I was manifesting on the inside.

A few years ago, I ran a two-day workshop in London. The room was buzzing with Lucky Bees who were meeting new friends and just excited to be there – and yes, excited to see me. I was seriously beating myself up for not losing my baby weight for the event. Willow was about a year old at that stage; and I was at least a dress size heavier than I had been before her birth.

I wanted to apologize to the audience:

- ✦ "I'm so sorry I'm not skinny for you."

- ✦ "I don't deserve to be standing up here in front of you."

- ✦ "I know that you're here to listen to my message, but I should be thin as well."

- ✦ "I'm sorry to let you down."

Were there people in the audience judging me? Maybe, but definitely not as hard as I was judging myself. Even when people were hugging and thanking me for my books, my weekly blogs, and the work I do, there was still a tiny part of me that was trying to suck in my stomach for the photos, and worrying that they would say to their friends afterward, "OMG, I went to see Denise, and she was so *fat*!"

It wasn't enough that I was a successful author and businesswoman. It wasn't enough to bring together two hundred women (and one guy) for a night of inspiration. There was still a niggling sense that I just wasn't enough.

I'll be honest: I sometimes still think that way; and if you do, too, then it's okay. We don't have to have perfect thoughts about ourselves to be successful.

But the difference now is that I show up anyway, despite not being perfect. Even if I sometimes have to *force* myself to make videos and do speaking gigs despite not being a "perfect weight."

I allow myself to wear beautiful, expensive clothes now… and I allow the money to flow into my life, even though I'm not perfect. I do it for me, and I do it to inspire other women as well. I want people to think, *If Denise can do it, so can I!* And honestly, I challenge you to be a leader for your community, too.

Don't worry: it's not that I think I'm some hideous troll. In fact, that's exactly why I wanted to admit that I feel this way. *So many women do* – and it's usually a completely BS story based on internal crap that makes no sense!

Practicing self-love and acceptance has made all the difference in my life, and it will completely change your fortune, too. I deliberately use the word "practice" there because, like most personal development, it's life-long work. Some days will be easier than others – and *that's okay.*

I mentioned the importance of getting your boobs on board in Chapter 3. Just think what you'll be capable of when you practice deep self-love and acceptance for your entire body!

I used to look at women who were naturally slim and vibrant, and think, *You lucky bitch!* I always struggled with my weight, even as a kid.

But it was more than that. I felt sluggish, unmotivated, and constantly tired. I had terrible self-talk. I wanted to have the energy to do all the awesome things I dreamed of, but my body couldn't keep up with my brain! When I look back at myself as a teenager, I really wasn't fat – but I was convinced that I was defective in some way. Yes, I had hips earlier than my friends, but that didn't mean I was fat and disgusting.

In truth, my self-blame and shame held me back much more than any actual weight problems (which were largely self-imagined).

Total self-love is your birthright. It's about you living your best life, feeling healthy and confident, and knowing 100 percent that you deserve it – no matter what that means for you: whether it's creating a really fit, athletic body; or dressing beautifully for your figure.

It's not about losing weight, or *not* losing weight. It's about loving yourself unconditionally, and then consciously *choosing* what you want to create in your life. And seriously, how sexy is that confidence that comes from within? It's irresistible and *attractive* in all senses of the word (especially from a manifesting point of view).

The key to manifesting anything comes down to how you feel about yourself and what you think you deserve. This will have a knock-on effect to almost everything else in your life. You get what you think you deserve.

As always, you can learn to tip the odds in your favor. And self-love is the secret to making it happen.

Why is self-love so important?

To be honest, in my experience, self-love is the *only thing* that helps women to transform their lives. I truly believe that if all you get from this book (or any of my work) is that you're allowed to love yourself, your life will be transformed. Love yourself now. Exactly as you are.

You have permission.

You are enough.

That's honestly it. Yes, I talk about other topics, but they're just the surface stuff. Almost everything I do has the underlying message of, "Hey – you're okay. You're enough. This is normal. You can do this!" (Of course, you might get bored if that was all I taught, so I have to dress it up in different clothes to brainwash you from all angles!)

People ask me all the time what I'm going to teach to my kids – as if I know anything about raising humans! I don't. I'm sure I'll make lots of parenting mistakes, and they'll end up being their own people.

But if all I can teach them is to *practice* self-love and acceptance – well, everything else will fall into place. That's why I teach them Emotional Freedom Technique (EFT). I'm trying to positively brainwash them from an early age into believing that they're okay. That they're enough. That's all. That will give them a valuable skill set, and then they can figure out the rest.

Many women who struggle with self-love feel like major failures; and this can spill over into other parts of their lives. For some people, it's in their business. For others, it's their relationship (or lack thereof). And for some women, the story is around weight and money!

Can we talk about weight and money?

Weight seems to be a taboo topic in personal development. Can you be fat and successful? *Can you be fat and rich?*

Can you have a little extra "junk in your trunk" like I do, and still make money? Is that even allowed? Funny question, isn't it? But I seriously used to think this way.

Because I didn't know many rich or successful people in real life back then, I only saw them in movies and on TV. And ALL of them were very thin.

I internalized quotes like, "*You can never be too rich, or too thin,*" which is commonly attributed to Wallis Simpson, Duchess of Windsor. That or, "*Nothing tastes as good as skinny feels,*" by Kate Moss. So even though I was gaining success in my business, there was a part of me that said it didn't count unless I was skinny, too.

Now, in our reality TV culture, we still associate having money with being extremely thin. We repeatedly see what happens when a "regular-sized" woman gets bashed and shamed in magazines for not having a thigh gap, or for having an extra tummy roll.

All these messages contribute to the self-hatred that lots of young women feel. The messages also set up expectations that unless we have perfect bodies, we're not entitled to other good things in life. Things like being successful, being in awesome relationships, or even simply just liking ourselves.

The last time I checked, there was no weight requirement for being wealthy and making money. Success doesn't have a weight limit!

However, I see a *lot* of female entrepreneurs really hiding their true selves, and repelling money because they're not happy with how they feel in their bodies. If you do this, you might resist getting new photos, because you think, *I'll just wait until I lose that last twenty pounds.* You might even say, "I've put on weight recently, so I'm going to push back my launch. That way, I don't have to be on camera."

I also see a lot of female entrepreneurs hiding behind really outdated brands, or sabotaging income opportunities because they're always *waiting* to be perfect.

You know how many of my blog readers have told me I'm fat? *Zero.* I've literally never had a single person send me a message to say, "Hey, I like your videos; but if you just lost a little more weight, I'd like them more!"

It's *never happened.*

But when you wait and wait and wait, you keep delaying your success. It's really not about your weight: that's just a BS excuse! It's not about your body. Get honest and realize that it's mostly about self-love, and not allowing yourself to reap the benefits of your hard work now.

★ *Lesson* ★

Money blocks affect people of all shapes and sizes. Success comes to people of all shapes and sizes.

So your weight could be a complete big, fat (haha) excuse for not creating the business that you love. Now I don't know about you, but every time I look back on old photos where I thought I was totally fat at the time, I realize that I actually looked smoking hot.

Admit it honestly: even if you weighed less, your life wouldn't necessarily be happier, and your money blocks would still be there. If it wasn't your weight, it would be your accent, or your skin, or your education. You'd just find another excuse for not taking action toward your dream life.

If you got skinny or lost those "last twenty pounds," you'd still have your money blocks. If you won the lottery, you'd still have your money blocks. Success *isn't* hiding behind extra rolls of fat on your body.

So here's the good news.

You can totally be as rich and as fat or skinny as you like. There are no rules. You're perfectly ready exactly the way you are right now, and you deserve to create an amazing business *and* all the elements of a First-class life.

So, how do you get to the place of self-acceptance? How do you clear these old habits and form a new relationship with your body?

How do you *honestly* cultivate self-love?

Own your past

We always go back to our origin stories! It's powerful to understand what may be holding you back from feeling good in your skin and creating success now. To clear the slate and fall effortlessly in love with yourself, you need to get clear on where you've come from, identify why you've failed or succeeded in the past, and put all those old stories to rest.

When you take the time to analyze your past, you'll often see patterns that were holding you back, some of which were completely out of your control.

Start by simply writing down your body/health/weight story. After that, it works the same way as any other forgiveness exercise: release any old resentments with love, understanding, and forgiveness.

This is an essential exercise because you can get really deep and dirty, and describe your struggles in vivid, compelling detail. It's only for you, so you can get really clear on what's been holding you back until now. You just need to be completely honest with yourself, and remember: you don't have to share this with anyone.

You might find that your patterns are crystal clear, or you may need to do some further probing. If you have a sympathetic friend, telling them (if you're comfortable doing so) can often uncover themes that you weren't aware of.

When I did this, I asked myself, *If how you do anything is how you do everything, how does success relate to my relationship with food?*

Holy shizzle.

There were so many parallels:

❖ I was never comfortable with having money in my bank account, because it felt like a waste. I felt that if I had "extra," I should give it to others. I felt guilty having time off, because I felt lazy. Extra time felt like a waste.

❖ At the same time, I always overate at buffets, anxious to get my "money's worth," but never really being present or savoring the meal. If I had extra food on my plate, I felt guilty, like it was a waste – so I stuffed myself with food that should have gone into the garbage bin. And I went through feast and famine cycles where I either ate 100 percent raw food, or total junk food: nothing in between.

❖ I was the *exact* same way with money. If I got a windfall, I'd "eat" it all quickly, because who knew when I'd have spare money again? (This was directly related to an old family memory – more on that in a moment.)

Food was love. Food was a treat. Food was a punishment.

Have you ever gone on a shopping binge? My binge focus was food. I always had to eat everything on my plate, so I ate and ate… and ate without feeling satisfied. It never felt enough. I stuffed in food for a variety of reasons – because I was bored, tired, sad, mad, or just wanted a way to make myself feel better.

And here's the thing: when I first started my business, work never felt enough either. If I got one new client, I felt like it "didn't count" until I got two. But then that didn't feel satisfying either.

That same "not enough" feeling is what keeps entrepreneurs pulling all-nighters and never taking holidays. You might think, *When I earn X amount,* **then** *I'll feel successful!* but the success is an ever-moving target.

I felt so jealous of friends who could eat whatever they wanted, didn't overeat, and had great bodies… And with money, I felt jealous of friends who earned great money in their businesses, and could spend it with ease on nice things. I thought they were just "lucky," and that I'd never have a healthy relationship with money, especially since I'd grown up poor. Plus, I wasn't "allowed" to be successful in business because I wasn't thin enough.

Deep down, I thought I could only be rich when I was skinny. Otherwise I didn't deserve it.

So I sabotaged my income and I sabotaged my health. But honestly, they were both a lack of self-love, nothing else. And I had to get honest with some of my past behavior around how I treated my body.

For example, when I was younger, my idea of a fun treat was to go to an all-you-can-eat Pizza Hut. You might think I'm exaggerating about that, but I could sit there for hours; and I even went there to celebrate my 26th birthday! I absolutely loved pepperoni pizza: I couldn't get enough, so I would eat and eat and literally never feel full. I could eat much more than male friends, and I'd come out with my stomach straining, but always feeling like I could fit in just one more piece... In fact, I often snuck a few pieces away in a napkin to eat in the car.

For my twenty-eighth birthday, I had afternoon tea at the Ritz Hotel in London. It's a beautiful and memorable experience that you *have* to do if you're in London (the Dorchester is amazing, too). It's also a fancy kind of all-you-can-eat event because the waiters keep topping up your scones and sandwiches for as long as two hours! Well, I just couldn't stop.

We were the last people left in the dining room, and we kept taking more and more "free" sandwiches. I hobbled to the toilet with a hugely swollen stomach, and could barely peel off my Spanx to pee! I was actually really sick that night, too – all due to overeating to get my money's worth, instead of just enjoying the experience.

Overeating until I was sick was a regular occurrence. I had a serious McDonald's addiction, and I'd always buy a packet of chips or crackers to eat on the way home from work, even if I wasn't hungry. I never developed an actual eating disorder where I purged or denied myself, but it was a huge problem all the same.

Why the gluttony? I thought I just liked food and that I was greedy. But I now know that I ate to make myself feel numb and to deal with areas in my life where I felt uncomfortable, such as working in a job I didn't love, or not dealing with my childhood resentments. My eating resembled a form of self-harm. Making myself lethargic from the food also let me stay in those situations because it allowed me to justify to myself that I didn't have the energy to change it.

When I got clear on my past, I realized:

❖ I was numbing myself with food whenever I was stressed or worried.

❖ I was using food as punishment or reward instead of self-nourishment.

❖ I was staying fat to justify bad situations in my life.

❖ I was beating myself up whenever I did something "bad."

❖ I didn't feel like I deserved to be thin.

My food issues were clear to see on my butt. My money issues, on the other hand, were somewhat more hidden underneath. Honestly, though, both issues came from the same place: a horrible feeling that I just wasn't good enough.

Having these realizations shone a light on my self-sabotage, and I gave myself permission to overcome both sets of issues at the same time. After all, if one shifted, the other might, too, right?

I decided to forgive myself for my actions around both food and money. I cleared my past. I decided that I *am* enough. I realized that there is always more (both more food and more money) when I need it. I did a shit-load of transformational work on myself…

And the results have been incredible.

Remember how I said in Chapter 3 that if I only had one personal development tool available to me, I'd choose forgiveness? That's because it works on *everything*. It's such a powerful tool to clear the decks, release old shame and blame, and give you a new foundation to choose something different.

Here's what happened when I forgave myself and others for the self-hatred of my body. It was subtle at first. I found myself saying, "I'm full now," and pushing my plate away (this had *never* happened to me in my life). Or, instead of automatically halving everything with my husband, I gave myself more suitably sized portions.

I stopped worried about eating everything, or that I'd never get fed again.

I rarely do second trips to the buffet now, and if I do, it's without guilt. I eat dessert only if I feel like it, and not because it's there. I've lost weight; and while I'm still not a skinny bitch, I feel happy, in control, and in love with my life.

The funny thing was that when I realized I didn't have to eat everything on my plate, I started feeling comfortable having excess money in the bank, too. I didn't feel the need to spend it all quickly (and feel equally guilty about it afterward).

Does any of this resonate with you?

✧ Action ✧

Journal about your self-love story.

Start with either your money or your weight/food story, and ask yourself questions like:

✤ What are your memories around your self-image?

✤ How do you act at an all-you-can-eat buffet?

✤ What words would you use to describe your relationship with either food or money: for example, indifferent, greedy, guilty, stuffed, anxious, scary, out of control, wasteful, scarce, unsatisfying, harmful, unhealthy, dysfunctional, in denial, broken?

✤ Do you eat/shop in secret?

✤ Do you hoard weight/money?

I have a few vivid memories that I want to share in case they spark something for you. First, when I was really young (maybe around six or seven), I overheard my mother talking on the phone to a friend. She said, "I just don't know how I'm going to feed them this week." Now, she might have been literally down to zero dollars in her bank account (likely), or her budget could have just been tighter than usual that week. Either way, I made a decision then and there. If there was food available, I was going to stock up, because who knew when I'd get fed again?

Now to be clear, there were never times in my life that I felt like we were so poor that we wouldn't eat. Yes, there were lots of cheap frozen fish fingers in my childhood, but we weren't destitute or scavenging through trash cans.

But that one memory made me fearful of "going without," and it was the start of my literal feast-and-famine relationship with food *and* money. You think I just liked pepperoni pizza? No, I was trying to avoid potential upcoming starvation – a story that a small child made up.

My second memory was in fourth grade. Our school teacher was weighing us. I can't remember why exactly – it might have been a school requirement or for a science lesson. Either way, I was really tall for my age back then. I stopped growing two years later at 5'4", but at that point I was taller than my classmates. And I wasn't a skinny tall child, either: I had more of a woman's figure. I definitely wasn't obese though, just puppy fat.

As my teacher weighed me, he said something like, "Wow, you're as heavy as an adult!" His words started my "story" that I was massively fat, that I had a huge weight problem, and that I didn't deserve to wear nice clothes or show my body in any way.

My last memory: a really popular guy I had a crush on in the eighth grade told me that he would totally go out with me... if I wasn't so fat. Again, I wasn't even that big! But of course, it set me on the path of believing that I didn't deserve love if I wasn't as skinny as other girls at age sixteen!

I share those three memories (and I have a million more) because you probably have similar ones of your own. You almost certainly have fairly innocuous situations in your past that you've turned into "facts" to support the highly destructive hypothesis that you're not allowed to be successful, happy, loved, wealthy, confident, etc.

Forgiveness allowed me to clear those memories. And now, as an adult, I don't have to eat everything in sight, because I'm no longer that fearful seven-year-old, that shamed ten-year-old, or that spurned sixteen-year-old. (By the way, I saw that guy at a party years later, and he was a total loser!)

Once you've written down your list of memories, what do you do with it? Go through each one, use the forgiveness mantra again, and cross the memory off your list. This is the work that will keep giving in every area of your life.

And if body issues aren't your thing, that's okay – the process works on everything. Find another area of your life that you're struggling with, and tackle that instead.

Love and accept your body now

Before you can receive all the external trappings of success, you need to really, truly love yourself, as you are now.

If you have an inner voice that constantly tells you that you're too fat, too short, or too ugly, you'll find it hard to make traction in other areas of your life. Why? Your negative self-belief will be like an invisible force field, shielding you from receiving money, love, good health – really anything on your dream board.

Maybe you'll only be a vibrational match to other people who, deep down, feel the same way about themselves: unworthy of love and success. This could show up in the type of clients you attract, or it could keep you stuck with friends and mastermind buddies who drag you down.

There are many ways you can retrain your subconscious to love and accept yourself. Forgiveness, as I've outlined above, is a brilliant tool; but it's not just about forgiving other people. You can forgive your body, too. (Remember: my philosophy is always to come at it from as many different angles as possible.)

Every cell of your body has to be on board the self-love train.

I teach the same thing on my Money Bootcamp; and honestly, I'd teach it with any other subject, too. You have to be energetically aligned to your goals. Otherwise you'll always repel what you think you want. You don't even need to be 100 percent aligned – just more often than not. Perfection isn't necessary.

The best way to get every cell in your body aligned to your love goal is to lose the emotional charge around your physical reality. Accept yourself from the ground up.

If body acceptance is something that you really struggle with, and you feel a lot of shame, blame or self-hatred for your body, your homework is to do this exercise every single day with the intention that you'll love yourself first, no matter what. It's the first step in attracting the life you want to experience, because the Universe will mirror what you already feel in yourself.

★ Lesson ★

Accept yourself as worthy
and others will, too.

In this particular exercise, we're going to get your toes on board, your ovaries, your skin, your hair: every single part of your body is going to be moving in the same direction. Even if you don't have a specific goal in mind, this practice will help you to feel worthy in every cell of your body.

The annoying paradox about the Law of Attraction is that the Universe can only give you what you've already got, or what you already feel. That's why, when you feel broke, you manifest a parking ticket; or when you've got a giant pimple, you run into a hot ex-boyfriend. The aim is to make you feel so loved and grateful that the Universe can't help but match your vibration.

This is otherwise known as the self-fulfilling prophecy. If you expect something with every fiber of your being, you'll attract it, whether it's more money or a new lover. That's really the only hard thing about conscious manifestation. You have to feel it before you see it, which requires the internal work first.

Using tools like forgiveness helps you to come to peace with your own body, and makes sure that every cell of your body is on board with your dreams. If your underlying program of "I'm not good enough" is running the show, you'll activate the self-fulfilling prophecy that you don't deserve good things to happen to you.

It honestly doesn't matter whether you're manifesting money, a soul mate or new clients, the body forgiveness work is equally important, and incredibly easy.

Body shame will derail your goals

I often hear Lucky Bees in my Bootcamp say, "But Denise, why is it important to love my body to make more money?"

The answer is that if you have self-hatred and shame at a cellular level, you'll never allow yourself to manifest anything amazing in your life.

That is the truth.

Body shame is not a new thing, but it's been amplified over the last couple of decades by advertising, sexy music videos, reality TV shows, and even the popularity of everyday people having plastic surgery. No wonder we feel so bad about ourselves when we're faced with a barrage of images that tell us that we're only beautiful if we look like celebrities.

I remember watching an Extreme Makeover marathon. By the end of it, I was studying myself in the mirror and cataloguing all my faults. Of course that kind of mentality and self-criticism will impact other areas of your life.

I want to let you know that, no matter what weight you're at now, no matter how you feel in your body or how you think you look, you can still manifest a First-class life. No exceptions.

The body love process

Grab your journal and a pen. Don't get distracted and go off to do something else. I know there's definitely a temptation to procrastinate on this type of work, particularly when you don't want to look at something because it will make you feel uncomfortable.

So you might feel like going and grabbing something out of the fridge, or distracting yourself with your phone, but I just want you to stay with it, because this is going to make a huge difference to your self-esteem and self-love. Truly accepting that you're a lovable person and that you deserve good things starts with you.

It starts with how you feel about yourself.

Start with a personal inventory of your body and how it makes you feel. Be very clear and very honest, but don't judge or criticize yourself. That's not the intention of this exercise at all.

Instead, you want to get clear on how you feel about your body and the unspoken judgments that you have all the time about how you look and feel in it. Think about every bit of it – your toes, your skin, your boobs, your nose…

1. Take a self-love inventory

This exercise will open your eyes to how you're treating yourself, and how much self-love you have in your life. First, download the self-love inventory sheets at the bonus page, www.DeniseDT.com/bonus.

Next, go through the inventory. As you do, try not to be overly critical of yourself. Just write down what you think and feel about each body part in turn, and pay attention to what that part of your body is trying to tell you. Maybe there could be a twinge or a problem. Maybe there's something that you need to deal with.

Write down the first thing that pops into your mind. It could be a negative word like "fat," "hairy," "disgusting," or "cellulite." Or it could be something positive, like "beautiful," "soft," "silky," or "sexy."

There's no right or wrong. It's only about awareness, so just write down the first thing you think of for each part.

Inventory *every inch* of your body, starting from your toes all the way up to your hair, and everything in between. Note down your feelings and judgments.

For some body parts, you're going to have nothing to write down. That's great, but most of the time, people identify at least one or two areas of themselves and their body that they've been seriously neglecting. That is highly symbolic to the Universe.

For example, when I was a kid in primary school, another kid told me that I had a flat face. He said that I must have gone down a slippery slope and landed flat on my face, and that it stayed that way. I looked in the mirror every morning after that and studied my face. I couldn't tell what he was talking about, but then a few other kids went, "Yeah, Denise has got a flat face."

I had a complex about my face for a long time when I was growing up, and all because some stupid kid just made an insult up. That complex definitely held me back from dating or being confident in my career, because I was convinced I had some sort of serious facial deformity.

You'll probably remember a few things like that, or notice parts of your body that you're ashamed of – things like scars, stretch marks or "imperfections." I was pretty shocked the first time I did this exercise – it was clear that I had very negative feelings toward myself. And remember:

it's hard to consciously manifest when you disapprove of yourself at a cellular level.

Imagine saying, "You're so stupid! You never get anything right!" to a little kid. Or maybe saying, "You are so fat!" to your mother! You wouldn't do it, right? So why accept it when you do it to yourself?

This exercise isn't designed to make you feel worse about yourself. We're just shining a light on your negative programming. Then, when you clear and release that programming, you allow yourself to receive more in your life.

My manifesting ability improved a thousand-fold when I stopped beating my body up for not being perfect. I changed the underlying program. Yes, of course, I still have moments of self-criticism; but it's not my dominant program anymore, so I don't sabotage my goals.

2. Make peace with your body

Once you've completed the self-love inventory, it's time to start making peace with your body, by doing the same forgiveness mantra I outlined earlier in the book. I like to do my body forgiveness work just before I go to bed. If you struggle to fall asleep, this exercise will relax you and make you feel amazing. Imagine what would be possible in your life if you completely and utterly loved and accepted your body no matter what?

I also do this exercise whenever I feel any blame, shame or self-criticism about my body. I just stop myself in the moment of criticism, and say the forgiveness mantra.

You're going to be shocked by how much judgment you have about almost every single part of your body. When you think of it from an energetic perspective, is it any wonder that you haven't achieved all of your goals?

Sometimes it's really disgusting how we talk to ourselves. But now's the time to be super-careful with how you treat yourself, so that you show the Universe how you want to be treated – in a positive way, not a negative, hateful one. This is such a crucial part of manifesting your First-class life, because your complete self-love will have a ripple effect throughout the Universe.

"I finally realized that being grateful to my body was key to giving more love to myself."

OPRAH WINFREY

Here's a recap on how to do body forgiveness. Close your eyes, and in a relaxed frame of mind, go through each of your body parts in turn and say the forgiveness mantra. This time, you're not forgiving other people – you're forgiving yourself (which is honestly a lot more powerful anyway, because we as women harbor so many negative feelings toward ourselves and our bodies).

Go through each part of your body a second time; and this time, as you think about that part, say the forgiveness mantra.

"I FORGIVE YOU.
THANK YOU.

I'M SORRY.
AND I LOVE YOU."

Say, "I forgive you," to let each part of your body know that you accept it with all its flaws, and that you accept yourself for not being a supermodel and not being perfect.

Say, "Thank you," to acknowledge the lesson you've learned, and that your body has been supporting you your whole life, even though you've treated it the way you have.

Say, "I'm sorry," to apologize for how you've treated your body. Maybe you've been neglecting it, demanding that it be different, or blaming yourself instead of having compassion.

Then you always finish with, "I love you," to send love and self-acceptance to every cell of your body.

The reason we do this exercise body part by body part is that we've accumulated so much shame and self-hatred that we need to make sure we root out as much of it as possible. So begin at your feet, and work your way up to your head. Soak in the love and forgiveness, and feel the weight come off your shoulders.

This is such a crucial exercise. You have no idea the ripples this will send out to the Universe: "Yes, she's ready to receive more!"

★ Lesson ★

Show the Universe you're ready for
more by loving yourself first.

3. Start practicing self-care

Additionally, I believe that one of the most *powerful* things you can do to love yourself is to replace dieting with extreme self-care. Think of self-love as the outcome; and self-care as the practical day-to-day actions that contribute to it.

Why stop dieting? For a start, I just don't believe that diets work. If they did, you wouldn't hear so many horror stories of women who've struggled for years through ridiculous regimes like the Atkins diet or the cabbage soup diet. And seriously, I tried so many funny diets myself that I should know! If you did, too, make sure you add all of those "failed attempts" to your forgiveness list.

Being rich and famous doesn't mean your diets will work either – even if you have a private chef and personal trainer. For example: it's well known that the Biggest Loser contestants struggle to maintain even an average level of exercise and diet after they leave the show. Some of the contestants are even taking legal action against the show because of alleged abusive and dangerous practices they endured, which they say have completely messed up their metabolism.

One of the world's most famous "failed" dieters, Oprah Winfrey, shares many stories about times in her life when her eating was completely out of control. One day she was so desperate for junk food that she threw some frozen buns in the oven and turned the heat up high to cook them quickly. She was so impatient that she ate them, burnt on the outside and frozen on the inside, and just covered them all over with maple syrup. This is a woman who's a *billionaire*. She could hire someone to watch her diet 24/7, and she has private chefs and personal trainers, but she suffers from the same problems as other women.

So don't pin your hopes for "a body worth loving" on yet another diet. Instead, focus on showing your body that you *already* love it by eating nourishing food that gives you pleasure (and keep doing your forgiveness work!).

Wouldn't it be awesome if you accepted that you're "good enough" the way you are now, and stopped beating yourself up for not being perfect?

Sort out any niggling health problems

Do you tend to ignore your physical self-care? I've been guilty of this myself – from the smallest thing like postponing a manicure (I actually have chipped polish today!) to "forgetting" to book my regular dental appointments. If you're like most people, you probably have a few niggling health problems that you've been ignoring. Some of them may have been caused by neglect, which means they can be prevented in future with a bit of self-care, exercise or long-overdue professional attention.

Start by making a to-do list of any practical health issues you need to deal with. For example, if your teeth hurt and you haven't been to the dentist for a while, add making an appointment to your to-do list. Ask yourself when you last had a Pap smear, gynecology appointment, or general check-up? Do you need to go to the chiropractor, acupuncturist or massage therapist? If so, put that on your to-do list as well.

The point is to take care of yourself as beautifully as you'd want somebody else to take care of you. Everything I ask you to do in this book is highly symbolic, and is a message to the Universe that you're ready to be treated like a queen who's worthy of a First-class life.

I once did a program where I had to complete a luxurious self-care activity every day for thirty days. It was eye-opening, and I was *shocked* at how I was treating myself. Some days I only wrote down "went for a walk" under self-care. Does that sound like a luxurious treat?

Important note: If there's something "wrong" with your body, don't take it as a sign that you're not "destined" to be successful; or that there's something wrong with you as a person. Don't wait until your knees are better, or until your back doesn't hurt so much, to start changing your life. Instead, use it as a *reason* to get better and to love yourself more.

What could you be taking care of right now, but find yourself resisting because of the time, money or anything else? Remember: these niggles are *highly* symbolic. You wouldn't ignore your kids if they complained about an aching tooth or a mystery pain. Instead, you'd sort it out for them. You'd never neglect an innocent child the way you neglect yourself, would you?

And by "neglect," I mean all the things in your body that you ignore or put up with. My physiotherapist says that he'll see someone who tells him they can't raise their arm above their head. When he asks how long the problem's been going on they say, "Oh, about ten years." *Ten years?* When something feels wrong, deal with it straight away!

There's usually a practical reason for it; and it *certainly* doesn't mean you're not worth loving.

Don't let budget issues hold you back from practicing self-care either. You only have one body. You'd find the money for your kids, wouldn't you? Some self-care practices don't even cost money, like spending an extra fifteen minutes on your makeup or hair each morning. If you can't be bothered doing it now, what makes you think you'll do it later?

Start treating yourself like a treasured child: someone who deserves the best love and attention. From a manifesting viewpoint, this sends a very clear message to the Universe that you're worthy of the highest levels of care and happiness. Nothing is too small to take care of (and actually, the small stuff is empowering because again, it means you come at manifesting from all angles). And most of it probably won't cost as much as you think.

So get practical. Revisit your body inventory, and see what you can put into action straight away. That might mean actually calling and making appointments, sorting out your health insurance, or just making sure that you take some time over the next day or two to do something that feels good for yourself.

Don't just think about "boring" maintenance stuff as you write your to-do list. Could you increase your pleasure threshold by getting a massage just because it feels good, and not because you "need" one? Could you read a book in a hot bath; or give yourself a home facial?

Then, once you have your list, pick *one* thing on it that you can do in the next five minutes. It might be calling to book a dental check-up, moisturizing your dry elbows (those poor bits always get neglected), or doing a long overdue breast self-examination.

Next, aim to do three things from your to-do list in the next twenty-four hours. For example, you might:

✦ Go to the dentist for your check-up

✦ Get your Pap smear done on time

✦ Check out that dodgy back pain

✦ Buy some awesome running shoes

Commit to completing any items that remain over the next month at most. Don't procrastinate and leave it any longer than that. If you have problems that you need to deal with, do so now!

You might be thinking, *Denise, what the hell has this got to do with getting new clients or making more money?!*

The answer is that it's *all* related. From an energetic perspective, you're laying the groundwork to have an incredibly different experience of receiving good fortune compared to what you're used to. My job is to help you transform your entire life – and that starts with how you treat yourself.

As you check items off your list, you're preparing yourself to create outrageous success, and taking yourself above and beyond what you're used to. You're not just getting through your to-do list!

Plus, the complaint I always hear about the Law of Attraction is that it's too complicated and esoteric. I'm an incredibly practical person, and I love giving you easy-to-follow exercises to become luckier. Dealing with your physical "stuff," i.e. your body, will have a huge impact on your manifesting ability.

> *"The happiness you feel is in direct proportion to the love you give to yourself."*
> OPRAH WINFREY

Love yourself in *every nook and cranny* of your body, take action to show the Universe you're ready for more, and you'll very quickly start manifesting anything you want. It's magic when that happens!

✧ *Action* ✧

Make your self-care list something you tick items off every day.

Extreme self-care makeover

Once you get the basics out of the way (and lots of us need to start there), you can go beyond regular body maintenance to see how much pleasure you can stand.

This isn't just about buying yourself flowers or going to the hairdresser to get your roots done. Instead, it's about allowing yourself time and space for things that bring you joy. Go above and beyond what you think you deserve, and do things that feel decadent – even lazy.

Again, these things don't have to cost a lot of money.

I love spending time in solitude, sitting in a beautiful space – either at home or in a park – and just reading and enjoying the beauty around me. Being in nature makes me feel good and healthy. But I also love getting weekly blow dries for my hair, and having quarterly spa days with my girlfriends. I used to feel like a "spoiled diva" for doing these types of things – but they've now become my new normal.

What about fun stuff? Do you feel guilty going to the movies on a weekday instead of working (why else go into self-employment in the first place)? Do you feel bad for lingering over a coffee on the weekend because you could use that time to write another blog post?

Sometimes when we're busy, fun things go out the window because we think we don't have time. When money's tight, we feel guilty about spending it on fun experiences. We have a million excuses, but basically, having fun for fun's sake feels frivolous!

The reason that taking time out is so important is that when we laugh and have fun, we feel lighter and happier. This spills over into every part of our lives. If you think about it from a manifesting viewpoint, having more fun puts you into a positive vibration.

✧ Action ✧

Reflect on how much fun you
allow in your life.

Get out your journal again and ask yourself:

✤ What do you like to do for fun?

✤ When's the last time you did any of these things?

✤ What's holding you back?

In case you need it, I officially give you permission to have fun! Do something just for the sheer fun of it. It might feel luxurious and spacious, and that's exactly the vibe you want to put out into the Universe.

> *"Getting my lifelong weight struggle under control has come from treating myself as well as I treat others in every way."*
>
> OPRAH WINFREY

Make a commitment to self-love

Before I started taking care of myself, I was never really connected to myself as a physical being. I've always lived very much in my head; but you can't have true success without acknowledging the fact that you *do* have a body and it deserves to be loved.

I can clearly remember the day I decided that I was going to commit myself fully to changing my life, including changing my career and releasing my money blocks.

Here's what was going on for me physically at the time: I was at my heaviest weight, and I didn't feel comfortable in myself. I didn't want to spend money on so-called "fat clothes," so I wore dull colors and second-hand clothing. I was stingy with myself to the point of embarrassment. I wanted to be a millionaire, but I couldn't even let myself window shop in nice stores.

Do you see the mixed message I was sending to the Universe?

I had recurring problems with my knees and back, so I was going to the physiotherapist all the time. I wouldn't commit to other treatments though, because I felt guilty about spending the money when Mark and I had a wedding to pay for.

I suffered from anxiety at work, which gave me itchy fits, constant sweatiness, and bad BO. My skin was dull, and my eyes were lifeless. Despite all of this, though, I was waiting for someone to make me redundant from a job that was sucking the life out of me, instead of taking positive steps toward starting my own business.

I'd been hospitalized two and a half years earlier with pneumonia, and I still felt physically weak. I'd get puffed climbing the stairs; and every time I got a cold, I worried that the pneumonia would come back. My body felt heavy and I knew I wasn't healthy.

Energetically, I wasn't great either: I constantly felt stressed and tired. Mark would try to encourage me to exercise with him, but I couldn't muster the energy. I just liked to lie around reading on the weekend. Work was grinding me down; and I found I was getting really negative – constantly bitching and complaining about work and my colleagues. I couldn't go on like that.

One day, I woke up and said, "No more."

I was ready for change.

What really helped me was to forgive myself for the mistakes of my past, and then forgive others so I could move on from the pain and decide that I was worthy of having an amazing life.

I started with little actions – like paying attention to my need to pee, instead of ignoring it so I could keep working; or – at the other end of the scale – making sure that I drank enough water. At the same time, I began to slowly shift my beliefs about myself, and tackled each negative belief, one at a time.

As I started taking better emotional care of myself, I also started to eliminate some physical problems. It was a big realization to me that I didn't have to *suffer*, and that life could be wonderful. The physical self-care, combined with the energetic work (like forgiveness), helped me to make the changes I needed to make.

From there, I started writing a blog, and believing that one day I could work for myself. When I developed higher standards for myself, I stopped tolerating some of my friends' negative attitudes. I started using my commute to read self-help books instead of catching up on sleep.

It all sounds small, but remember that small actions compound over time – and that's exactly how you create your First-class life.

> *"To me, good health is more than*
> *just exercise and diet. It's a point*
> *of view and a mental attitude*
> *you have about yourself."*
>
> ANGELA LANSBURY

Release your fears

A few years ago, I decided to work with a health coach who specialized in mindset work, because I knew that there was a missing piece for me that had nothing to do with food and exercise.

The most enlightening thing about our work together was uncovering my fears around being thin. I was afraid I'd become vain and shallow, or that I'd get unwelcome attention from guys. The biggest fear was that I wouldn't be relatable to my audience anymore! I literally said to my coach, "Nobody will like me if I'm thin *and* rich!"

Huge aha!

It's not surprising that I struggled to lose weight or allow myself to wear nice clothes. Holding on to the weight validated some of the excuses I used for not living my dream life!

✦ "Nobody will like me!"

✦ "My husband will leave me!"

✦ "I can't have everything!"

Have you ever been on a good run with your self-care, then suddenly sabotaged yourself with junk food and felt massive resistance to continuing? I used to feel so good after going to the gym that I went straight to McDonald's. It was like I couldn't handle the pleasure injection, and I had to dampen it down somehow.

Or what about self-sabotage in your business? Maybe you've had an awesome month, but then suddenly felt sick and started procrastinating? I remember back when I had my best income month ever, all I wanted to do was to sit on the couch and play Candy Crush on my phone. I told myself that my financial results were just a fluke and that I could never do it again.

This is incredibly common because suddenly, your success puts you in new territory, and you don't know how to act. You ask yourself, *Who am I if I'm incredibly successful? Who am I to have a pleasurable life?*

As much as we'd all like our dreams to come true quickly, we often have conflicting feelings, like guilt, shame, or unworthiness. This is completely normal.

★ Journal ★
What might happen if you started truly looking after yourself?

You might have a friend who's naturally skinny, but you think she's really vain and obsessed with her looks. You secretly judge her because of it… and you worry that *you'll* be vain, too, if you're skinny. So it's safer to stay the way you are. But that's *her* script, not yours; and you don't have to repeat it.

Or you might judge someone you know who seems to have an "easy life," or worry that getting your hair done regularly will make you a "snobby rich bitch."

The fear of success is an incredibly common phenomenon, but we never recognize it in ourselves. It's easier to think that we don't have the will power than it is to admit that we're scared of what life will be like when all our dreams come true. Our fear of the unknown seems to be stronger than the potential reward.

After all, if you've never felt rich, loved or healthy, how will you know how to act when you get there? You might struggle with the identity of the "new you." Who is she? What does she like? How does she dress or behave in public? How does she deal with the new attention from others?

You might fear that you'll act differently, that your friends won't like the new you, that some people might be jealous, or that you'll put your relationships in jeopardy.

Plus, sometimes our scripts are dictated by other people's reactions. Perhaps a friend once made a negative comment to you when you shared a business success or a new self-care ritual with her. Maybe someone's said, "Must be nice!" in a really bitchy way, and immediately made you feel guilty for treating yourself like a VIP.

You may worry that you'll become a completely different person or that others will view you negatively for loving yourself. A common fear is that you'll lose all your friends or become a total bitch. Don't worry, it's highly unlikely that you'll become a bitch (maybe a Lucky Bee!), but it's a very valid irrational fear.

Take out your journal, and write down the fears that come up when you think about all your goals coming true. Ask yourself: what's the *very worst* thing that could happen? Use the structure:

If I achieved this goal, I'm afraid that…

Acknowledging those fears is the first step in tackling them, because most of them will be completely irrational and silly. That means you'll be able to halt sabotage in its tracks because you'll know it's just a story that you're making up.

Be happy now

You don't have to wait until some perfect day in the future to get a manicure, or to buy a fabulous pair of shoes. There's never been a better time to love yourself.

So many women think, *Universe, send me the success, and* **then** *I'll act like a successful woman would*, or *Universe, make me perfect, and* **then** *I'll love myself!*

Nope, that's the wrong way around. If you knew that you deserved an amazing First-class life, how would you act? Think of that ideal version of yourself. Step into her shoes, act like she would, and make it real for yourself *now*.

This is a journey and a life-long process. There will never be a time when everything is fixed and perfect, because perfection doesn't exist.

Make your dream of self-love and acceptance so compelling and irresistible that you feel yourself living it more and more each day. The more you believe in your new, exciting vision, the more your current reality will feel like a temporary state, and you'll naturally start to act in the way that nourishes your ideal self.

Success breeds success; and small, regular, incremental changes lead to permanent and long-lasting transformation.

You deserve to love yourself... *Now.*

*"I always thought I should
be treated like a star."*

MADONNA

It's safe to grow and change

Give yourself permission to grow and change. As you become more "lucky," and take more responsibility for what you manifest, change will naturally seep into every area of your life. Old habits might start to feel strange. Old friends who don't serve you anymore might seem less appealing to hang around with. Places you used to go seem less fun. Honestly, this will happen in all areas of your Lucky Bee journey, no matter what goal you're working on.

These are all great signs that you're on the right track! It can be scary to feel like you're moving out of familiar territory, but it's 100 percent worth it!

You'll keep finding new layers to unravel, and new memories and layers of self-criticism to release. Write it down, forgive it, and move on.

You might feel scared to break out of the mold, but you can also step into a leadership role and inspire others. The bad news is that you might have to break up with some "friends" if they can't accept the new you. Embracing self-love can be really threatening to others, because it shows up their own lack of self-love. The good news, however, is that you'll attract new friends who appreciate you for who you are, and what you're doing with your life.

At this point, some Bees start to realize that all this newfound confidence and energy lets them do things they never thought possible. They might quit an unfulfilling job to start a new business, take up a new hobby, restart an old one, or embark on a creative project outside of work.

Whatever it is you want to do, you have the power. Just believe in yourself, and know that you can carry it through. The Universe has your back!

You're on your way to being the luckiest, healthiest, most loved version of yourself. At every stage, you can take it to the next level. You're not only worth it, it's your destiny.

It's your time, and you're ready for the next step.

CHAPTER SUMMARY

❖ Nobody judges you as hard as you judge yourself, and perfection is not the path to success.

❖ Self-love and acceptance is really the *only* lesson you need to learn. Everything else is a bonus.

❖ There's no weight requirement for success, and money blocks affect people of all shapes and sizes – so stop using it as your excuse.

❖ Clear your past, forgive yourself, and love yourself to success. Give yourself permission to attract everything your heart desires.

My Final Note to You

I first wrote this book because I was sick of my friends calling me a "lucky bitch" when I knew that it was not really luck, but a lifetime of self-development that created the circumstances for my life. Like many women of my generation, I was raised on Oprah and Louise Hay, and these remarkable women taught us how to love ourselves and break the cycle.

I hope you've been inspired by my story of how I won the Honeymoon Testers' competition, as well as how to implement all the practical stuff, too. Becoming an amazingly lucky manifestor is honestly not hard – you just follow the steps, clear your old beliefs and allow yourself to believe something amazing is possible for you, too.

Here's a reminder of all the actions in one handy cheat sheet. I'll add a printout to the free bonus package at www.DeniseDT.com/bonus.

Chapter 1: How I Became a "Lucky Bitch"

✤ Say out loud: "It's my time and I'm ready for the next step!" Be careful – it's powerful and the Universe will take it literally and send you an opportunity. Be ready for it!

✤ Write down your ideal day in the most vivid detail you can imagine.

✤ Listen to nudges from the Universe, and then actually act on them – like when my friend texted me about the competition.

✤ Try "faking" the feeling of excitement deep in your belly when you think about achieving your goals – even if it just feels like you're flexing your tummy muscles at first.

✤ BONUS: visit www.DeniseDT.com/bonus and download the Ideal Day Meditation.

Chapter 2: How I Became a Professional Honeymoon Tester

✤ Create anchors during positive experiences so that you can re-experience the same feeling later, and attract more of those experiences into your life (like I did in Bali on honeymoon).

✤ Write down your goals, and be as specific as possible, including how much you want (remember how I put a certain salary on my dream board and got the exact amount?).

❖ Don't keep your goals to yourself: tell your (positive) friends about your wildest dreams – they might have opportunities or ideas for you.

❖ If achieving your dreams requires applying for something, find out the deadline and put it in your calendar *now*. Then get the application in *early*.

❖ Visualize yourself having achieved your goal as often as possible.

❖ Turbocharge your affirmations by phrasing them in question form as afformations (from the book by Noah St. John).

❖ Make energetic space for your dreams by scheduling them into your calendar – make it real.

❖ Declutter any distractions to achieving your goal and deal with any practical considerations as early as possible.

❖ Dream boards work, so create one today.

❖ Check off every manifesting tip in the bonus action guide to make sure you're giving yourself the best chance of achieving your goal.

❖ Build your network before you need it.

❖ There's always more you can do, so do everything you can think of to guarantee your success.

✤ Brainstorm every potential "problem" that could keep you from achieving your goal, and solve it beforehand.

✤ If your goal involves applying for something, read the instructions carefully and then do the actual work! Most people won't bother.

✤ Keep believing you'll achieve your goal right up until the last second: decide right now that you'll never give up.

✤ Trust that the Universe might have a different path to the desired direction.

Chapter 3: The Ten Lucky Bitch Commandments

✤ Forgiveness: Write down everything you can think of that's still a painful memory, then use the forgiveness mantra on each one.

✤ Take the time to get really specific about what you're scared of, grab your journal, and write about your fears.

✤ Journal all the things you have to be grateful about right now.

✤ Start blocking out pockets of VIP "freedom time" to enjoy in your day. Plus, increase your pleasure threshold by dedicating at least 10 percent of your income to yourself for things that bring you pleasure.

- Do body forgiveness work, using exactly the same process that you used to forgive other people.

- Send out "positive love bombs" to other people each day.

- Actively decide to be a "reverse paranoid."

Chapter 4: Your Lucky Biz

- Journal about what you liked to do as a child to help you figure out your true calling.

- Ask yourself whether you're working to your strengths in your current business.

- Ask yourself whether you're unconsciously limiting your income to appease other people.

- Figure out what you're doing in your business that doesn't serve you, and make a plan to stop doing it!

- Journal your excuses for not being ready for the business of your dreams now.

Chapter 5: Abundantly Lucky (Get Rich, Lucky Bitch)

- Reflect on your basic money beliefs.

- Write down your money story.

- Write down what being a wealthy woman means to you.

* Write down the money messages that you're sending to the Universe.

* Clear your money blocks to receiving large sums of money. Start by thinking of any downsides to having a lot of money and being rich.

* Read *Get Rich, Lucky Bitch!*, or join my Money Bootcamp.

Chapter 6: Self-love Will Change Your Fortune

* Write down your own body/health/weight story, then release any old resentments with love, understanding, and forgiveness.

* Journal about your self-love story.

* Go through each body memory you identify, use the forgiveness mantra again, and cross the memory off your list.

* Write out a to-do list of any practical health issues you need to deal with.

* Once you have your list, pick one thing on it that you can do in the next five minutes; and three things that you can do in the next twenty-four hours. Then commit to completing everything else over the next month at most.

* Aim to tick items off your self-care list every day.

* Reflect on how much fun you allow in your life.

- Journal about what might happen if you started truly looking after yourself.

- BONUS: Visit www.DeniseDT.com/bonus and download the self-love inventory sheets and the self-love meditation.

Thanks for joining me on this journey!

My final message to you is… Why not you? Why not now?

It really is your time and you're ready for the next step. Love and luck,

xx Denise
www.DeniseDT.com

ABOUT THE AUTHOR

Michelle Swan

Denise Duffield-Thomas is the money mindset mentor for the new wave of online female entrepreneurs. Her best-selling books give a fresh and funny road-map to creating an outrageously successful life and business.

Denise helps women release their fear of money, set premium prices for their services, and take back control over their finances.

Denise is an award-winning speaker, author, and entrepreneur who helps women transform their Economy-class money mindset into a First-class life.

 DeniseDT

 DeniseDT

 DeniseDT

www.DeniseDT.com

HAY HOUSE
Look within

Join the conversation about latest products, events, exclusive offers and more.

f   Hay House UK

🐦   @HayHouseUK

📷   @hayhouseuk

💜   healyourlife.com

We'd love to hear from you!